The
Maltese

An Owner's Guide To

A HAPPY HEALTHY PET

Howell Book House

Howell Book House
A Simon & Schuster Macmillan Company
1633 Broadway
New York, NY 10019

Macmillan Publishing books may be purchased for business or sales promotional use.
For information please write: Special Markets Department, Macmillan Publishing,
USA, 1633 Broadway, New York, NY 10019.

Library of Congress Cataloging-in-Publication Data
Linden, Bobbie.
The Maltese/[Bobbie Linden]
p. cm.—(An owner's guide to happy healthy pet)
Includes bibliographical references.
ISBN: 0-87605-237-5
1. Maltese dog.   I. Title.   II. Series.
SF429.M25L55   1998
636.76—dc21   98-22378
            CIP
Manufactured in the United States of America
10 9 8 7 6 5 4 3 2 1

Series Director: Amanda Pisani
Assistant Series Director: Jennifer Liberts
Book Design: Michele Laseau
Cover Design: Iris Jeromnimon
Illustrations: Steve Adams and Jeff Yesh
  Back cover, front cover and inset photo by Paulette Braun
Photography:
Mary Bloom 30, 32
Paulette Braun 5, 11, 14, 17, 39, 41, 53
Bob Schwartz 6, 10, 13, 20, 33, 36, 43
Toni Tucker 8, 15, 21, 23, 25, 55, 59, 68
Judith Strom 12, 18, 48, 51, 63, 64, 65, 66, 75, 80
Cheryl Primeau 22, 34, 37, 57
Zig Leszczynski 19, 93
Production Team: Toi Davis, Clint Lahnen, Dennis Sheehan, Terri Sheehan,
  Donna Wright

Contents

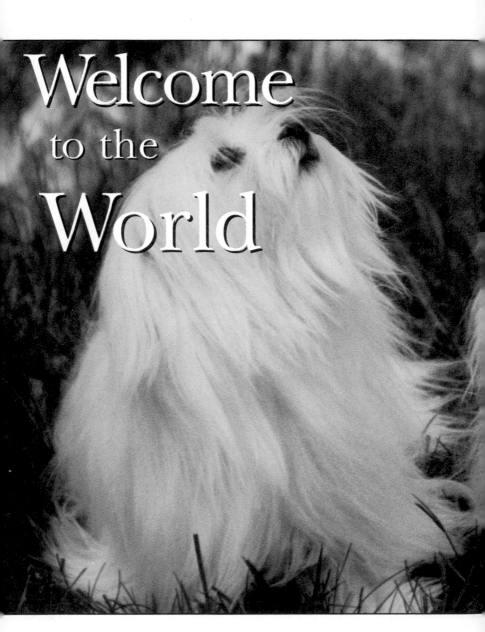

Welcome
to the
World

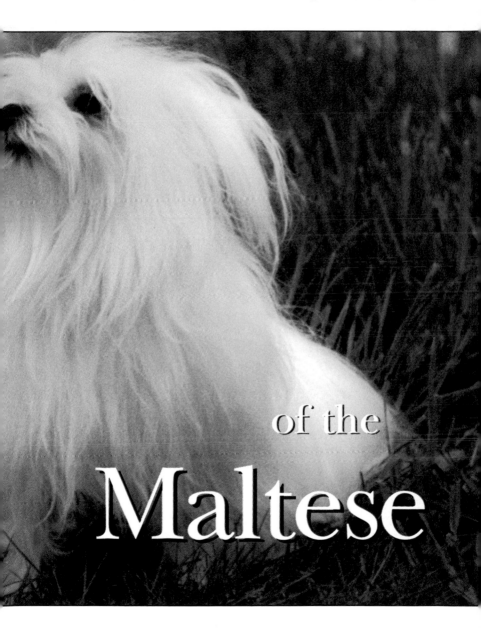

of the

Maltese

External Features of the Maltese

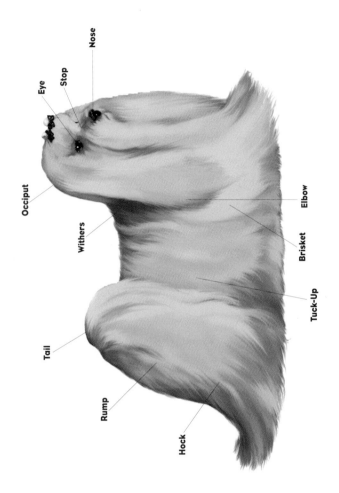

Nose

Stop

Eye

Occiput

Withers

Tail

Rump

Hock

Tuck-Up

Brisket

Elbow

chapter 1

What Is
a Maltese?

Known and admired for thousands of years, the lovely Maltese with their silky white coats have always symbolized elegance and beauty wherever they go. These little dogs are equally prized as a highly regarded show dog and a loyal, outgoing companion. While they are at home sitting gently by your side, they are also

playful, cherish a lively walk and can have an adorable mischievous streak.

What Is a Breed Standard?

All dogs come with four legs, a tail and a head with ears, eyes and a nose. So how do we differentiate a Maltese from other dogs? We use

5

something called a standard. This blueprint is a description in simple words that depicts the breed characteristics of a Maltese. (There is a standard for every purebred dog.) However, the standard can sometimes be difficult to fully understand and can, in fact, take many years of study to distinguish its finer points. Breeders, judges and fanciers use the standard as a yardstick by which they measure the quality of the Maltese. It should, however, be remembered that the standard describes the "perfect" Maltese. But no dog is ever perfect and no Maltese will possess every quality in the standard.

A Maltese should have eyes that are bright and clear, a coat that is healthy and well groomed.

Five Useful Tools To Judge Conformation to the Standard:

Type—Type refers to the combination of distinguishing characteristics that make a Maltese unique from another breed of dog.

Balance—Balance refers to the Maltese's overall proportions. A well-balanced Maltese will have no glaring faults or just one outstanding feature.

Style—Style refers to a combination of showmanship, personality and elegance. An outstanding Maltese should possess all of these traits.

Soundness—Soundness refers to the absence of any disability that interferes with the gait or movement of the Maltese.

Condition—Condition refers to the overall health and well-being of the Maltese. A Maltese should be neither too fat nor too thin. His eyes should be bright and clear, his coat healthy and well groomed.

Official Standard for the Maltese

The standard follows in italic type. An explanation appears in regular type.

General Appearance *The Maltese is a toy dog covered from head to foot with a mantle of long, silky, white hair. He is gentle-mannered and affectionate, eager and sprightly in action, and despite his size, possessed of the vigor needed for the satisfactory companion.*

The Maltese is distinguished from all other breeds of dogs as the only dog with a long, silky, white coat. The standard is very specific in specifying "silky." The coat should have the feel of a finely textured silk fabric, somewhat "cool" to the touch. The Maltese should be gentle in manner but still lively and vigorous. While he may enjoy sitting quietly by his owner's side, he still loves romp and play time. There should be no suggestion of terrier-type aggressiveness. The Maltese is a devoted companion to his master but at the same time should not be shy of strangers.

Head *Of medium length and in proportion to the size of the dog. The skull is slightly rounded on top, the stop moderate. The drop ears are rather low set and heavily feathered with long hair that hangs close to the head. Eyes are set not too far apart; they are very dark and round, their black rims enhancing the gentle yet alert expression. The muzzle is of medium length,*

WHAT IS A BREED STANDARD?

A breed standard—a detailed description of an individual breed—is meant to portray the ideal specimen of that breed. This includes ideal structure, temperament, gait, type—all aspects of the dog. Because the standard describes on ideal specimen, it isn't based on any particular dog. It is a concept against which judges compare actual dogs and breeders strive to produce dogs. At a dog show, the dog that wins is the one that comes closest, in the judge's opinion, to the standard for its breed. Breed standards are written by the breed parent clubs, the national organizations formed to oversee the well-being of the breed. They are voted on and approved by the members of the parent clubs.

fine and tapered but not snipy. The nose is black. The teeth meet in an even, edge-to-edge bit, or in a scissors bite.

The shape of the head and the features of the Maltese impart the adorable look that has attracted so many to the breed. There are two distinctive types of head of Maltese seen today. Although the Maltese is not a true spaniel, one type of Maltese has a head that resembles those of the spaniel group. The second type is more

suggestive of a terrier—with a longer nose, a narrower head and high-set ears. This second type is considered incorrect and serious Maltese breeders have worked hard to eliminate this type from breeding programs. The overall balance of the head must be kept in perspective to the standard.

Many Maltese fans use the term "halos" when describing a Maltese head. While the standard makes no mention of halos, they are a char-

"Halos" are defined as a darkening of the skin around the eyes.

acteristic that may enhance the overall appearance of the head. Halos are defined as the darkening of the skin around the eyes. Many times the presence of halos may be connected with good pigmentation, but there have been many outstanding specimens of the breed that do not have extensive halos.

"Black points" is another term used by Maltese admirers to describe the presence of black pigment on the eye rims, nose and toe pads.

Neck *Sufficient length of neck is desirable as promoting a high carriage of the head.*

The high neck carriage gives the Maltese the elegance that distinguishes it from other breeds of dogs. It should also be noted that to have the proper high neck carriage, the Maltese should possess proper layback of the shoulders and construction of the front legs.

Body *Compact, the height from the withers to the ground equaling the length from the withers to the root of the tail. Shoulder blades are sloping, the elbows well knit and held* *close to the body. The back is level in topline, the ribs well sprung. The chest is fairly deep, the loins taut, strong, and just slightly tucked up underneath.*

The appearance of the Maltese should be of a compact or "cobby" dog. He should be square from the point of the withers to the base of the tail and from the point of the withers to the ground. The ideal angle of the shoulders should be 45 degrees. Incorrect toplines will cause a Maltese's back to have a rounded appearance or be high in the high quarters. Any tendency toward flatness in the ribs is also incorrect.

Tail *A long haired plume carried gracefully over the back, its tip lying to the side over the quarter.*

The tail should be set high. A common fault with many Maltese is a low set tail that causes the dog to look longer than it should and destroys the compact appearance. A tail with a feathered appearance or that is carried above the horizontal is also a serious fault.

Legs and Feet *Legs are fine boned and nicely feathered. Forelegs are straight, their pastern joints well knit and devoid of appreciable bend. Hind legs are strong and moderately angulated at stifles and hocks. The feet are small and round, with toe pads black. Scraggly hairs on the feet may be trimmed to give a neater appearance.*

The Maltese is one of only three toy breeds to mention fine bone in the standard so it is important that this characteristic be present. The Maltese is a fine, delicate dog that originally was a "sleeve-dog" of the aristocracy. To maintain this position in the early times it

---

The American Kennel Club

Familiarly referred to as "the AKC," the American Kennel Club is a nonprofit organization devoted to the advancement of purebred dogs. The AKC maintains a registry of recognized breeds and adopts and enforces rules for dog events including shows, obedience trials, field trials, hunting tests, lure coursing, herding, earthdog trials, agility and the Canine Good Citizen program. It is a club of clubs, established in 1884 and composed, today, of over 500 autonomous dog clubs throughout the United States. Each club is represented by a delegate; the delegates make up the legislative body of the AKC, voting on rules and electing directors. The American Kennel Club maintains the Stud Book, the record of every dog ever registered with the AKC, and publishes a variety of materials on purebred dogs, including a monthly magazine, books and numerous educational pamphlets. For more information, contact the AKC at the address listed in Chapter 13, "Resources," and look for the names of their publications in Chapter 12, "Recommended Reading."

was important that they retain this fineness. Any suggestion of large bones and a larger size is still a serious fault.

The issue of black toe pads has caused some controversy in recent years among Maltese breeders. Some have suggested that the pigmentation of these points is separately inherited and many have no relation to pigment of the other points on the head. In spite of these opinions the breed standard has not been changed and it is still a requirement that the toe pads be black.

*The Maltese
coat is long,
flat and silky.*

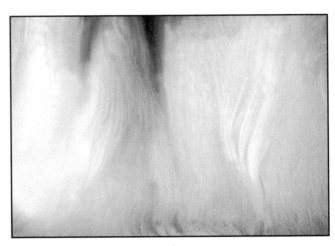

Coat and Color   *The coat is single, that is, without undercoat. It hangs long, flat, and silky over the sides of the body almost, if not quite, to the ground. The long head-hair may be tied up in a topknot or it may be left hanging. Any suggestion of kinkiness, curliness, or woolly texture is objectionable. Color, pure white. Light tan or lemon on the ears is permissible, but not desirable.*

There is probably no sight more remarkable than the elegant Maltese floating around the ring with his white coat flying. The remarkable coat is, perhaps, what makes these lovely little dogs stand out from all others. A true "silky" coat is one that falls flat to the body. Unfortunately, many Maltese seen today do not possess this silky coat but have coats that have been made to appear silky using numerous coat preparations and grooming techniques.

Maltese in the United States are typically shown with two topknots that are known to some as "horns." The appearance of these topknots is enhanced by the use of small bows usually in a dark color. Puppies are many times shown with a single topknot, as their headfall may not be long enough to be placed in double topknots. Maltese in Europe and Australia are generally shown as an adult with a single topknot.

Many Maltese will have blackish or grayish patches on the skin of their bodies and sometimes will have tan colored coat growing from these areas. Some breeders equate these patches with good pigment, but it is just as common to see heavily pigmented dogs that are pure white. It is entirely possible that the dark patches are evidence of the colored Maltese that were bred in the early 1900s.

Size   *Weight under 7 pounds, with 4 to 6 pounds preferred. Over-all quality is to be favored over size.*

The standard is very clear on the issue of size. Maltese are toy dogs and the size must be maintained in this range to meet the overall balance and elegant appearance of the breed.

Gait   *The Maltese moves with a jaunty, smooth, flowing gait. Viewed from the side, he gives an impression of rapid movement, size considered. In the stride, the forelegs reach straight and free from the shoulders, with elbows close. Hind legs to move in a straight line. Cowhocks or any suggestion of hind leg toeing in or out are faults.*

The Maltese is a toy dog and should weigh between 4 and 6 pounds.

Sometimes it is difficult to assess the movement of a Maltese in full coat. However, an educated eye can usually spot some of the serious faults such as dogs with limited reach and drive—demonstrated by an appearance of wasted energy in their locomotion. Other faults to look for include paddling (swinging the front

*The Maltese is
lively and
playful.*

legs forward in a stiff arc), crabbing (moving with body at an angle of the front), single tracking of the rear legs and hopping. Hopping can be suggestive of problems with loose kneecaps or loose knee joints on the rear legs.

Temperament *For all his diminutive size, the Maltese seems to be without fear. His trust and affectionate responsiveness are very appealing. He is among the gentlest mannered of all little dogs, yet he is lively and playful as well as vigorous.*

The Maltese personality is unique among the many breeds of dogs. The temperament of the Maltese is probably one of his most outstanding characteristics. A Maltese that is shy or overly aggressive should be considered to have a serious personality defect.

Standard Approved March 10, 1964

chapter 2

The Maltese Ancestry

Known to many as "ye ancient dogee of Malta," the Maltese can be traced back many centuries. This beautiful silky-coated little white dog has a rich and exciting history. The admirers of Maltese come from all walks of life from the pet fanciers and show fanciers to the rich and famous. Few breeds have achieved such affection and admiration over the years as the elegant little Maltese.

Early History

Many believe that the Maltese originated on the Isle of Malta in the Mediterranean Sea. However, it is argued in Miki Iveria's *The Jewels of Women* (published by the Maltese Club of Great Britain) and other sources that the Maltese actually originated in Asia. Evidence of dogs resembling the Maltese have been found in ancient drawings, art and writings from as early as 5000–2000 B.C.

Some experts contend that the Maltese was brought to the Mediterranean from Asia.

Assuming the place of origin of the Maltese to be Asia, the tiny dogs probably made their way to Europe through the Middle East with the migration of nomadic tribes. The Isle of Malta (or Melita as it was known then), was a geographic center of early trade, and explorers undoubtedly found ancestors of the tiny white dogs left there as barter for necessities and supplies.

References to the little white dog are made in early European writing. In describing a breed of small dogs, Aristotle likens them to the "Canis Melitae . . . of the tiny sort, being perfectly proportioned not withstanding its very small rise." The Maltese were favorites of the Greeks and Romans of old. There are many drawings in existence portraying small, longhaired dogs on pieces of Greek and Roman pottery. During these times the Maltese was a favorite lap dog of fashionable men and women about town, being carried wherever its master went.

The ancient Europeans long held the belief that the small dogs came from one of the islands off the coast of Sicily, hence the name Canis Melitae (eventually geographers and writers agreed to the name Malta). The Maltese is one of few dog breeds to have retained its name from its known origins.

Malta's location made it an important place in the Mediterranean. It developed a culture and a race of people with distinctive characteristics, and it developed the little Maltese, a race of dogs that differs from almost every other breed. Malta's geographic situation provided an ecology that remained undiluted by outside influences for many centuries. Maltese, as dwellers of the island of Malta, were bred as purebred dogs as far back as the early 1500s.

The English Background

Maltese were first imported into Britain during the reign of Henry VIII, and they became great favorites in the time of Queen Elizabeth I. By the middle of the 19th century, the breed was well established as a pet dog in Britain, and when dog shows began, the Maltese were featured among the early exhibits. Many of the Maltese in the U.S. today trace their heritage back to English imports.

Many of the Maltese in the United States can trace their heritage back to English dogs.

The Maltese in the United States

Maltese were first seen in the United States around the late 1800s, but the geographic origin of these dogs is unknown. We do know, however, that the Maltese lines in the U.S. today resulted from the importation of the breed from Great Britain, Canada, Germany, France and Italy.

Members of the breed were participants in the earliest versions of the Westminster Kennel Club shows in the 1870s. Registrations with the American Kennel Club studbook in that time frame were made on the basis of show winnings. The first registrations of Maltese occurred in 1888, when "Snips" and "Topsy"—both bitches—appeared in the studbooks.

Formation of the American Maltese Association

The first club for Maltese, the Maltese Terrier Club of America, was organized in 1906. By 1917 the club was known as the National Maltese Club and held its first specialty show.

Two Maltese clubs were in existence by the end of the 1950s. The Maltese Dog Club of America was formerly the National Maltese Club and the other club was the Maltese Dog Fanciers of America. These two organizations merged in 1961 and formed the American Maltese Association.

WHERE DID DOGS COME FROM?

It can be argued that dogs were right there at man's side from the beginning of time. As soon as human beings began to document their existence, the dog was among their drawings and inscriptions. Dogs were not just friends, they served a purpose: There were dogs to hunt birds, pull sleds, herd sheep, burrow after rats—even sit in laps! What your dog was originally bred to do influences the way it behaves. The American Kennel Club recognizes over 140 breeds, and there are hundreds more distinct breeds around the world. To make sense of the breeds, they are grouped according to their size or function. The AKC has seven groups:

1) Sporting, 2) Working,
3) Herding, 4) Hounds,
5) Terriers, 6) Toys,
7) Nonsporting

Can you name a breed from each group? Here's some help: (1) Golden Retriever; (2) Doberman Pinscher; (3) Collie; (4) Beagle; (5) Scottish Terrier; (6) Maltese; (7) Dalmation. All modern domestic dogs (*Canis familiaris*) are related, however different they look, and are all descended from *Canis lupus*, the gray wolf.

The first president of the American Maltese Association was Dr. Vincenzo Calvaresi. One of the early tasks of the new organization was to ratify and submit to the American Kennel Club a new standard for the breed, which it did in 1963. This standard was approved by the AKC in March of 1964 and is the same standard in use by the breed today.

The first American Maltese Association national specialty show was held in June 1966. The AMA sponsors a national specialty show each year (usually in one of the summer months) rotating from the Eastern U.S. to the Midwest and the West on a three-year cycle.

Some Maltese Who Made History

The first Maltese champion recorded by the AKC was Ch. Thackery Rob Roy, owned by Mrs. C. S. Young, whelped in 1901. The first Best In Show winner is reported to be Ch. Sweetsir of Dyker in 1912, owned by Mrs. Carl Baumann.

In the 1950s, Toni and Aennchen Antonelli (Aennchen's Maltese) were the main force in establishing the Maltese breed in the U.S. One of the best known Maltese from their breeding program was the lovely female Ch. Aennchen's Poona Dancer, winner of thirty-seven Best In Shows and owned by Larry Ward and the late Frank Oberstar. For Maltese, the top Best In Show record of forty-three wins was held for many years by Ch. Joanchenn's Maya Dancer, owned by Mamie Gregory. This record was retained until the 1990s.

The Maltese became very popular in the 1950s.

The Maltese Today

The number of Maltese registered with the AKC grew slowly until the 1950s. Since then, however, the breed's popularity has increased dramatically among breeders, fanciers and pet owners. In the 1990s, the breed ranks in the top fifteen of all breeds with more than 12,000 Maltese registered annually. Maltese are one of the most popular breeds among spectators at dog shows, and they do not let down their many fans. They are frequent winners of the Toy Group in which they are shown and have an excellent record in Best In Show competition. The Best In Show record was broken in the 1990s by the lovely male Ch. Sand Island Small Kraft Lite, bred and owned by the late Carol Frances Andersen, who amassed eighty-two Best In Shows. Henry, as he was known, was the winner of the Toy Group at the Westminster Kennel Club show, as well as ranking as one of the top ten dogs of all breeds in the U.S. while he was actively shown.

FAMOUS OWNERS OF MALTESE

Elizabeth Taylor

Liberace

Billy Rae Cyrus

Tara Lipinski

Totie Fields

John Davidson

Lee Remick

Mia Farrow

17

Why do Maltese fare so well in the show ring? Some would say that their charming personalities make them natural (irresistible) winners. Others would argue that the advances in grooming techniques and grooming products have served to bring out the best in this adorable breed. Both of these factors may come into play, but is it undoubtedly the care taken by breeders to produce dogs of the finest quality that supports their fine performance.

The Maltese are an easy breed to train. This Maltese obeys a stay signal in an obedience competition.

Maltese in Obedience Competition

Maltese are seen less frequently in AKC Obedience competition than conformation events. Nonetheless, they are an easy breed to train and many owners have enjoyed the competition of earning a CD (Companion Dog) title and CDX (Companion Dog Excellent) title. As an indication of the im-portance of obedience competition, it is an event that is always included with the AMA National Specialty and several of the re-gional Maltese specialty clubs.

chapter 3

The **World** According to the **Maltese**

The Maltese is a very special sort of dog, with the spirit, heart and loyalty of a much larger animal contained in a very small body. Anyone who has become acquainted with a well-bred member of this breed has a respect and affection for its attributes and its history. This spirited little breed is very intelligent, sensitive and responsive. Most of all they are extremely loving.

What You Can Expect From a Maltese

Your Maltese will want to be your constant companion. He will be happy sitting by your side while you read a book or watch television, but he will also like to accompany you wherever you go. Maltese enjoy a walk with their owners, and a trip in the car is always welcome. They make good watchdogs and will sound alarms when a stranger comes to the door— but once the "stranger" is welcomed into the home, the Maltese will make friends with your guest. In fact, many fans of the breed have said that "they will kill you with their kisses" and "they would go home with strangers."

*You can expect
your Maltese to
retain his play-
ful and mischie-
vous nature.*

Maltese, despite their diminutive size, are a very hardy dog. Compared to many breeds they are quite free of genetic or congenital medical problems (see chapter 7). Your Maltese will live well into his teens and you can expect him to be his same playful and mischievous self for most of those years.

Maltese are one of several long-coated breeds, but they are the smallest and the only one with a pure white coat. The coat strongly resembles human hair and people who may be allergic to other breeds of dogs or cats may find that they can get along just fine with a Maltese. They do not shed their coats seasonally like dogs with short coats but because of their long hair they do require more maintenance than a shorthaired dog. Owners should expect to provide frequent grooming sessions or regular visits to a professional groomer.

Sunshine and Fresh Air

Sunshine is good for the overall health of your Maltese. All dogs need to go outside daily for fresh air. If you don't have a fenced yard or an exercise area, a walk around the block on his leash will give your dog his needed daily outside exercise. But caution should be used when walking a Maltese. He is such a friendly, fearless little dog that he will probably want to greet other dogs that he meets, and he could certainly be hurt by a less friendly canine.

The Maltese enjoys fresh air and sunshine.

Many people are concerned about the pigment (or lack thereof), on the nose of their Maltese. When noses turn grayish, fade or have patches of white at the corner, they are sometimes referred to as "winter noses." Breeders and exhibitors have long known that the more time a Maltese spends outdoors "soaking up" the sunshine, the deeper and darker the nose pigment. While you should ensure that your Maltese has plenty of fresh water while he is out and that the temperature is not exceedingly hot, he will enjoy some time lolling in the sun "working on his nose tan."

CHARACTERISTICS OF THE MALTESE

Elegant

Loyal

Friendly

Hardy

Delicate

WINTER WALKS

Maltese love to walk, day or night, winter, spring, summer or fall, even in the rain or snow. If you plan to walk when the weather is inclement you should consider investing in a sweater and/or raincoat for your Maltese. Tiny doggy boots are also available to protect little feet in extreme conditions. As if a Maltese was not adorable enough on his own he is probably even more adorable with his sweater on. And his sweater or raincoat will help him enjoy his frequent excursions.

*Put a sweater
on your Maltese
when you take
him out in cold
weather.*

Not a Playmate for Small Children

Maltese are definitely entertaining little characters, and with their love of people and small size many children are naturally drawn to them. Bear in mind that although a Maltese may look like a stuffed toy, he is not. Maltese can break —if you have children that want a dog to roll and play with on the floor, you may wish to consider a different breed. Because of their delicate bone structure they can easily break bones falling off chairs, tables and when caught in the middle of a pile of overly zealous children. In fact, many reputable Maltese breeders will not sell puppies to families with children under 6 or 7 years of age.

The Maltese and Other Pets

Because of their lively personalities, Maltese usually get along well with most other animals in the household. But do remember that your Maltese will probably be the smallest dog in the home and you may need to supervise a rambunctious larger dog closely when playing with a Maltese. Maltese are also without fear regarding these larger dogs. On a lead in a strange environment, a Maltese will more often than not have no fear approaching the larger dog. Do be careful as this larger dog may not return the affection.

Maltese will get along well with cats in the household, but care must be taken with cats as well. A cat may choose to use her claws in play which can cause severe damage to the eyes of a tiny Maltese. Older cats sometimes need to be watched closely with a new Maltese puppy as they can consider them prey, much like a small rodent. As the Maltese matures and knows how to approach the cat this problem should be alleviated.

Take Your Maltese with You

Maltese, as adoring little companions, love to travel with their owners. The easiest and safest way for your

Maltese to travel with you is in his crate. If you will be going on a trip for an extended period of time remember to take a few of his favorite toys, his food and water dishes, a collar and leash and his food. Taking some of your home water along in a bottle can eliminate diarrhea that may be caused by changes in water. Alternatively, you can use a squeeze of lemon in the water to help alleviate problems associated with water away from home. Don't forget you doggy first aid kit (see chapter 7) and any medications he may take.

The easiest and safest way for your Maltese to travel with you is in his crate.

Welcome to
the World of
the Maltese

If you will be flying with your Maltese, he will need to visit his veterinarian to acquire a health certificate, insuring his vaccinations are up-to-date and that he is healthy. A Maltese can travel in the cargo hold for a small charge, but traveling in this area of the plane can be un-comfortable and frightening. Your dog will be much happier and safer traveling in a soft-sided specially de-signed pet carrier that most airlines allow in the passenger cabin. Make sure you check with your airline when making your travel plans and indicate that you will be traveling with your Maltese. While on the air-plane in the passenger cabin, your Maltese should remain in his car-rier. He will most likely spend most of the trip sleeping from the hum of the engines. Don't forget to take his traveling needs mentioned in the paragraph above.

Pet Maltese Should Not Be Bred

Many people, when they first become aware of this lovely breed, soon come to the conclusion that it would be a wonderful idea to buy a female puppy and to breed her, with the objective of ultimately making a nice profit. It is, however, nearly impossible to make money breeding dogs. There are so many things that can and do go wrong, and the heartbreak associated with this is best avoided. Many times Maltese females cannot deliver their puppies on their own and require a dangerous Caesarean section. If the female survives this surgery, her milk may be scarce, and thus the puppies will need to be raised by hand, requiring round-the-clock feedings every three hours. If your female is your only Maltese and she survives and is able to raise her family she will be busy with them for nearly two months and you are no longer the center of her attention. Your faithful companion now has other interests. Are you willing to give up the companionship of your Maltese for that period of time?

Many Maltese need Caesarean sections to deliver puppies, and your female Maltese will have a full-time job raising her puppies. Think very hard about the possible consequences before you breed your Maltese.

An even better reason not to breed your Maltese is to avoid exacerbating the problem of the abundance of abandoned dogs. One need only go visit some of the animal shelters to see the overly-bred pet population. Maltese are very rarely seen in shelter populations and have retained their breed elegance by dedicated breeders that know and understand the breed standard. Understanding the standard and the genetics in the breed may take many years. Not understanding the standard and haphazard breeding practices may lead the Maltese breed to deteriorate to a "me too" breed that is over-bred and ends up in shelter populations. This is not what you want for the Maltese, or for any breed of dog.

More Information on Maltese

National Breed Club
American Maltese Association
Pamela G. Rightmyer, Corresponding Secretary
2211 S. Tioga Way
Las Vegas, NV 89117-2735

Welcome to
the World of
the Maltese

The AMA can give you information on all aspects of the breed, including names and addresses of breed clubs in your local area as well as a breeder referral list. The club maintains a site on the internet at http://www.americanmaltese.org for club information, news and schedules of club sponsored events. The club publishes a newsletter entitled the *Maltese Rx* to which fanciers can subscribe. For information about the *Rx*, as well as membership information please contact the corresponding secretary.

BOOKS

Abbott, Vicki. *A New Owner's Guide to Maltese*. Neptune City, NJ: TFH Publications, 1997.

Arden, Darlene. *The Irrepressible Toy Dog*. New York: Howell Book House, 1998.

Berndt, Robert. *Your Maltese (Your Dog Books)*. Denlingers Publishing, Ltd., 1975.

Brandlyn, James, and Lori Wahlers. *Guide to Owning a Maltese: Puppy Care, Grooming, Training, History, Health, Breed Standard*. Neptune City, NJ: TFH Publications, 1997.

Brearley, Joan. *The Book of the Maltese*. Neptune City, NJ: TFH Publications, 1984.

Camino Book Co. Staff. *Maltese Champions, 1952–1989 (Breeder's Reference Series)*. Camino Book Co., 1992.

Camino Book Co. Staff. *Maltese Champions, 1990–1994 (Breeder's Reference Series)*. Camino Book Co., 1995.

Cutillo, Nicholas. *The Complete Maltese*. New York: Howell Book House, 1986.

Di Giacomo, Kathy, and Barbara J. Bergquist. *Maltese*. Neptune City, NJ: TFH Publications, 1997.

Fulda, Joseph. *Maltese: A Complete Pet Owner's Manual*. Hauppauge, NY: Barron's Educational Series, Inc., 1996.

Herrieff, Vicki. *The Maltese Today*. New York: Howell Book House, 1996.

Nicholas, Anna Katherine. *The Maltese.* Neptune City, NJ: TFH Publications, 1984.

MAGAZINES

The Maltese Magazine
Reporter Publications
P.O. Box 6369
Los Osos, CA 94312

VIDEOS

Maltese—VVT507, The American Kennel Club

Living
with a

part two

Maltese

chapter 4

Bringing Your Maltese Home

The first weeks that your Maltese puppy is with you will be busy and demanding. There may be times when you wonder if getting a puppy was such a good idea. Things will go well if you have patience and keep your sense of humor. Remember that puppyhood only happens once. The extra effort you put into it now will pay off in the future.

Preparing for Your Puppy

Before you bring a new puppy into the house, there are some key items that you should have on hand.

CRATES

Long ago, when dogs were still wild animals, they often slept in dens—shallow holes they dug in the ground hidden away in places where they felt safe from predators. A "crate" is just a modern version of a den. Just as you enjoy having your own room where you can go for peace and privacy, your dog likes having her own room, too. As well as giving her a safe, cozy place to stay, crates can make training your dog a lot easier. Housebreaking goes much faster when you use a crate and destructive chewing becomes easier to control. Traveling is safer for both you and your dog when she's in a crate.

The most popular crates are made of plastic or heavy welded steel wire. Plastic crates are lightweight, portable and are easily disassembled for storage or travel. Some of them come in decorator colors. Most plastic crates meet federal regulations for airline travel. Wire crates are also very popular and depending on your dog's needs, may be a better purchase than plastic. Look for sturdy crates with heavy gauge wire that are easily folded down into a "suitcase-style" shape for transportation and storage. Although wire crates are not approved for airline use, they offer better ventilation than the plastic types.

A crate need only be big enough for the dog to stand up, turn around and lie down comfortably. The crate should be large enough for your Maltese to stretch out on her side to sleep.

BEDDING

When your puppy first comes home, she will need a lot of rest following her exuberant and playful excursions in her new environment. It is important to find a place for the puppy's bed that is out of the mainstream of the household traffic that will allow her to get the rest she needs. If you have purchased a crate for your puppy, the crate makes an excellent bed. The addition of a washable, soft pad should make the crate a cozy bed that your puppy may prefer for years to come.

PUPPY ESSENTIALS

Your new puppy will need:

food bowl

water bowl

collar

leash

ID tag

bed

crate

toys

grooming supplies

Look for crate pads that are made of silky fabrics.
Cottony and woolly fabrics can cause static electricity
and contribute to breakage of coat on the ends. If your
puppy will sleep in a bed other than a crate, do not
purchase one made from wood or wicker, as your
puppy might chew on these materials and harm
herself. Look for beds made of the same silky type of
fabrics as those for the crate pads.

*Find a quiet
place in the
house for your
puppy to sleep.*

LEASH AND COLLAR

Your Maltese will need a leash and collar. Leather and
metal collars do not work well on Maltese due to the
long hair around their necks—a metal collar can catch
in the coat and the leather ones can wear it down. A
thin, nylon one-piece collar seems to work best for this
breed. Many of these have a ring at one end to which
a leash can be clipped. Select a leash that is made from
a similar, lightweight material. As an alternative, many
Maltese owners prefer to use the loop type one-piece
show leashes that have a slip knot closure. These
leashes can be purchased from many of the catalog pet
suppliers as well as at dog shows.

WATER AND FOOD DISHES

You will need small, lightweight bowls for food and
water. These can be made from metal, plastic or a
ceramic material. Many Maltese fanciers avoid using

plastic bowls as there have been indications that they may be a cause of staining of the facial hair.

Your breeder will let you know the food your puppy was eating and it is wise to continue feeding the pup the same type of food, so as not to cause stomach upsets. If, over time, you want (or need) to change your dog's diet, do it by adding a little of the new food at a time. With their long coat, Maltese that drink water from water dishes get wet and sloppy faces. The wet facial hair can be a breeding ground for yeast, which in turn cause tear staining. Many Maltese owners will offer their pets water from a water bottle such as those used for rabbits to alleviate this problem.

TOYS AND CHEWIES

Relatively small toys are best for a Maltese. Look for squeaky and inter-active toys. Maltese seem to particu-larly like the fuzzy, plush, soft toys as well as the latex chewable ones. The latter are great for exercising gums, and puppies like to chew! Notably, Maltese seem to want to chew on paper as puppies, and one solution to this is to give them an empty toilet paper roll to carry around. A "nutritious" toy many enjoy is a mini-carrot or a piece of vegetable. Maltese are very inquisitive lit-tle pups. It is wise to have a good supply of toys for your puppy or she is sure to find her own—and you never know what she will drag out of your closet.

Lightweight leashes and col-lars are best for a Maltese.

Identification

Owners of purebred show and breeding dogs have long used tattoos to comply with the rules of identifi-cation of the American Kennel Club and to provide permanent, visible identification should their dogs get lost. Many pet owners also tattoo their dogs for identi-fication purposes. A tattoo is etched on the inside of the dog's thigh near her abdomen.

A recent addition to the identification of dogs is the microchip, a tiny transponder the size of a grain of uncooked rice. This is a permanent identification system implanted under the dog's skin and read by a chip scanner. Implantation is done with an injector that places the chip under the loose skin at the dog's shoulder. The process to implant the microchip is quick and no more painful than a vaccination, the number is unique and the owner's name and address are available on regional or national data bases so a dog can be returned quickly and safely.

Puppies like chewable toys— and you want to encourage your Maltese to chew on her toys, not your shoes!

If neither of these options appeal to you, be sure to get your puppy a simple ID tag to attach to her collar. Your name, address and phone number should appear on the tag. (Many dog lovers contend that it is best not to have a dog's name on the tag, because being able to use the dog's name is advantageous to thieves.) If you do choose to tattoo your puppy, or to have a microchip implanted, you may want to the dog to wear an ID tag nonetheless. If someone were to find a lost pup, this is undoubtedly the first, if not the only place, that the individual would look for identification.

Puppy-proof Your Home

Raising a puppy is a lot like raising small children— they get into everything. Some of what they get into can be hazardous to their health or to your possessions.

You can make life safer for the puppy and your furniture by getting rid of hazards and temptations ahead of time.

To a puppy, the world is brand new and fascinating. She is seeing it all for the very first time and absolutely everything must be thoroughly investigated. Puppies do most of their investigating with their mouths. Murphy's Law says that a puppy will be most attracted to the things that are either the most dangerous to her, or the most valuable to you—electrical cords, the fringe on your expensive oriental rug or your brand new running shoes.

Preventing destructive and dangerous chewing is much easier than constantly trying to correct the puppy. Look around your home and think carefully about its contents. Check for objects that could, and should, be put up out of the way of a curious puppy. To make immovable items such as furniture unappealing, a spray of Bitter Apple can be applied to the legs. You may also want to use a little Bitter Apple spray on the woodwork around your floors. If there are rooms your puppy should be restricted from entering until she is well trained and more reliable, install a baby gate or keep the doors to those rooms closed.

Take a walk around your yard looking for potential hazards. If your yard is fenced, check the boundaries and gates for openings that could be potential escape routes. A Maltese puppy is very little and can work her way through a remarkably small hole in a fence. The grass is always greener on the other side of the fence—even to a puppy. If your yard is not fenced, make a resolu-

HOUSEHOLD DANGERS

Curious puppies and inquisitive dogs get into trouble not because they are bad, but simply because they want to investigate the world around them. It's our job to protect our dogs from harmful substances, like the following:

IN THE HOUSE

cleaners, especially pine oil

perfumes, colognes, aftershaves

medications, vitamins

office and craft supplies

electric cords

chicken or turkey bones

chocolate

some house and garden plants, like ivy, oleander and poinsettia

IN THE GARAGE

antifreeze

garden supplies, such as snail and slug bait, pesticides, fertilizers, mouse and rat poisons

*A little Maltese
puppy can get
herself through
a remarkably
small hole in
your fence!*

tion right now that your puppy will never be allowed to
run off leash without close supervision. Keep her safe
by keeping her on leash.

Create a Space for Your New Pet

Decide where you will put the puppy's crate, and have
it set up and ready for her arrival. Where to keep the
crate will depend on what's most convenient for you as
well as the puppy's response. Many puppies don't like
to be isolated in one part of the house while their family is in another, but some puppies won't settle down in
their crates if there's too much activity going on
around them. You might have to experiment with different locations until you learn what works best for
both you and the puppy.

Visit Your Veterinarian

Make an appointment with your veterinarian to give
the puppy a complete checkup within 72 hours of your
purchase. If you do not have a veterinarian, ask the
breeder or local kennel club for a recommendation.
Although the puppy has most likely been health-
checked by the breeder, an examination is additional
security against health problems. Bring along your
pup's vaccination history and arrange a schedule for

completion of her initial series of vaccinations. If your veterinarian offers microchip ID implants, this an excellent time to get one. You should also discuss with your veterinarian plans for spaying or neutering your puppy when he or she is older.

Use a Schedule

Work out a schedule for you and the puppy. Housetraining is much easier when the puppy's meals, exercise and playtimes are on a regular schedule throughout the day. Plan your housetraining schedule and create a game plan before the puppy arrives. It is strongly advised that you bring your puppy home on a weekend (and if possible, take a week or two off), in order to devote extra time to settling in and housetraining those first few days.

A puppy should be taken to her relief spot frequently—and she must have a chance to go out first thing in the morning and right before bed.

FEEDING YOUR PUPPY

Generally, puppies should be feed three times a day until they are 3 months old. They should be then feed two times a day for the rest of their lives. If you are feeding a dry kibble you may wish to soak the kibble in water to soften this for younger puppies. By the time they are 3 to 4 months old they should be eating the kibble dry or with a little canned food mixed in. Do not give your puppy fresh milk. If you have problems getting your puppy to eat, you may consider adding a little cottage cheese or some baby food meats to her kibble. (See chapter 5 for a thorough discussion of feeding and nutrition.)

HOUSETRAINING YOUR PUPPY

Effective housetraining begins with a schedule. A puppy should be taken to her outside relief spot right

37

before bed and first thing in the morning, as well as after meals and naps, and she should be praised when she does her duty. When taking the puppy to her outdoor spot, don't play with her or allow the children to do so. First things first. If the pup does not relieve herself, put her in the crate for a few minutes, then try again. Most puppies will not soil in their crates if they can possibly help it. Take your young puppy out every hour to the "potty" area, regardless of whether she has eaten. Over time, the puppy's bladder control will increase, and she can be taken out less frequently. If she doesn't urinate or defecate within 10 minutes, bring her inside and place her in her crate for 10-15 minutes, then try again. Continue this routine until she is successful, and then praise her. The times that a puppy will most likely want to eliminate are after eating or drinking, after a nap or after a period of play or vigorous exercise. Be patient, consistent and regulate what goes into your puppy's tummy, so you can regulate what comes out.

USE YOUR BREEDER AS A RESOURCE

Use your puppy's breeder as a valuable resource for advice and information. Don't be afraid to ask questions. The breeder wants your relationship with your puppy to be successful and can offer many tips based on years of experience.

Many Maltese owners live in apartments and have found that they prefer to train their puppies to the disposable pads such as those used in hospitals, which have a plastic backing. Puppies train well to these pads and many use these for their entire life.

Never punish your Maltese puppy for mistakes. If your puppy does have an accident, don't spank, scream, or push her nose in the mess. The spot should be cleaned up, preferably with an enzyme odor eliminator. If the odor is left untended, the dog will find it again, even if people cannot detect any smell. Failures in housetraining are human mistakes, not puppy errors. The puppy does not understand that carpets are for walking, not bowel relief.

If a puppy reaches 4 or 5 months of age and is still having regular accidents in the house, make sure that she does not have a bladder infection, intestinal parasites or other medical reason for her failure to signal that she needs to go outside. Then redouble the efforts to teach her what you want her to know.

It is important that you check your puppy's rectum daily as stool can get stuck in her hair and prevent her from having a bowel movement. Obviously, this can cause serious problems and be very painful. Trimming the hair around the rectum will help keep her clean and healthy.

Socializing Your Puppy

Because your new puppy will quickly grow up, you should start socializing her the minute that you bring her home. Decide what rules you want obeyed, and stick with them from day one. Inconsistent rules do not work. If you don't want your Maltese to beg while you eat, never feed her from the kitchen or dining room table, and do not feed her right after you eat. By feeding your Maltese before you eat, feeding her in a place away from where you eat and requiring her to remain away from the table while you eat, your puppy will become a polite dog. Consistency is essential. By allowing your pup to eat up a piece of food dropped on the floor during your meal, you undo your previous work.

If you don't want your adult dog to jump onto your bed, don't allow your puppy to do so.

If you allow the puppy to jump up onto people when she's little, she will do it when she is an adult. If the puppy sees what life is like from on top of a chair or bed, she will be at home there when she's an adult. Decide what rules you want the adult dog to obey in your house and apply them to your puppy now. Be consistent.

Exposure to new environments, situations, people and animals is all part of the socialization process. If your dog has had limited exposure to the outside world start slowly, keeping in mind that it may be stressful for your dog. Gradually add distractions and new locations. Socialization is like any other part of training, building on small successes to make the foundation strong. Reward your Maltese when she exhibits relaxed behavior, by using treats, praise, petting or play. Make a list of all the places you can take your dog and start bringing her with you. (For an extensive discussion on how to train your dog, see chapter 8.)

chapter 5

Feeding
Your
Maltese

Every living thing needs protein, fats, carbohydrates, vitamins, minerals and water to live, but the quantities of each nutrient vary with the amount of physical or mental stress placed on the organism. For example, in order to replace the water lost due to perspiration, athletes need to drink more water than nonathletes. Young puppies need relatively more nutrients than adults do; moderately

active adults need more nutrients than those who are sedentary; and malnourished or sick Maltese need more nutrients to regain health.

Canine Nutrition

In addition to protein, fats and carbohydrates, dog foods also must contain vitamin and mineral supplements in balanced concentrations. Too much of one mineral may interfere with absorption of another; too little of a mineral may interfere with vitamin use or other mineral use. Major dog food companies make every effort to provide balanced proportions of vitamins and minerals for maximum benefit to the dog.

A Maltese will thrive if fed any one of several dry dog foods, depending on his level of activity, his metabolism and his individual body chemistry. In order to maintain a healthy coat, many owners find that Maltese do best on a diet that is high in protein and fat content. If your Maltese is doing well on the food you are feeding, do not switch food. If your dog has skin problems that cannot be traced to an obvious cause such as fleas, consider a food with a higher fat content or one of the hypoallergenic foods.

Understanding Nutrients

Nutrients are chemicals ingested by living organisms that are necessary for survival. The six basic nutrients needed by living things are protein, carbohydrate, fat, vitamins, minerals and water. Fats, carbohydrates and water are made of carbon, hydrogen, and oxygen molecules in different configurations; proteins include these elements and nitrogen.

HOW TO READ THE DOG FOOD LABEL

With so many choices on the market, how can you be sure you're feeding the right food to your dog? The information's all there on the label—if you know what you're looking for.

Look for the nutritional claim right up top. Is the food "100% nutritionally complete?" If so, it's for nearly all life stages; "growth and maintenance," on the other hand, is for early development; puppy foods are marked as such, as are senior foods.

Ingredients are listed in descending order by weight. The first three or four ingredients will tell you the bulk of what the food contains. Look for the highest-quality ingredients, like meats and grains, to be among them.

The Guaranteed Analysis tells you what level of protein, fat, fiber and moisture are in the food, in that order. While these numbers are meaningful, they won't tell you much about the quality of the food. Nutritional value is in the dry matter, not the moisture content.

In many ways, seeing is believing. If your dog has bright eyes, a shiny coat, a good appetite and a good energy level, chances are his diet's fine. Your dog's breeder and your veterinarian are good sources of advice if you're still confused.

Minerals are themselves elements; vitamins are complex chemicals of different composition necessary for various life processes.

PROTEIN

Proteins are chemicals made up of other chemicals known as amino acids. Dogs manufacture some amino acids in their bodies and must be supplied others in their food. Proteins from animal sources—meat and meat byproducts—are more complete and easier to extract and digest than proteins from plant sources. Proteins form the enzymes that metabolize food into energy as well as the hormones that guide various body functions. They themselves can also be metabolized to provide energy. High protein feeds are recommended for puppies and working dogs, but too much protein can cause renal (kidney) disease and has been implicated in some temperament problems.

Puppies need a diet that is high in protein.

FATS

Fats are probably the most misunderstood of the nutrients, for they are popularly considered the cause of obesity. It's true that a food high in fat will cause obesity in a dog that has a low expenditure of energy, because fats are higher in calories than either protein or carbohydrates. However, fats are essential for a dog's good health, particularly of the skin. Today's

43

homes are well-heated and have dry air that can exacerbate dry skin conditions. You may want to look for foods that include Omega fatty acids to help keep your dog's skin pliable and healthy. You can also add Omega fatty acids to your dog's diet as a supplement, but check with your veterinarian before supplementing your pet's food.

Fats increase the palatability of food, provide a media for fat-soluble vitamins, and affect food storage. They are also essential for reproductive efficiency and kidney function.

CARBOHYDRATES

Carbohydrates should comprise about 50 percent of a balanced food for dogs. The source of carbohydrates is an important consideration; corn is the most popular choice, with soybeans a close second. Other sources include rice and wheat. As long as the carbohydrate source is clean and of good nutritional quality, it probably does not matter which carbohdrates your dog eats. Some dogs may be allergic to one or more of these sources (some dogs may experience bloating or flatulence on soybean formulas), but most dogs do well on most sources of carbohydrate.

VITAMINS

Vitamins and minerals are necessary for proper absorption of fats and carbohydrates and for the chemical reactions in the body. Not only do organisms need these nutrients, but they need them in proper amounts and ratios for optimum health. For example, the right balance of calcium and phosphorus is necessary for these minerals to be properly absorbed and utilized. Failure to consume the right balance can lead to bone or muscle problems.

Some dogs may need vitamin or mineral supplements at given times during their lives. Some breeders give extra Vitamin C to dogs recovering from injury and boost bitches with Vitamins C and E during pregnancy. However, dogs manufacture their own Vitamin C, so supplements may be redundant.

Dogs with dry skin may benefit from daily doses of Vitamin E, and dogs under stress or bothered by fleas or biting flies may improve if given Vitamin B complex.

Vitamins are divided into fat-soluble and water-soluble types. Water-soluble vitamins are excreted from the body if they are not used; fat-soluble vitamins are stored in fatty tissue.

Among water-soluble vitamins are the B complex, including thiamin, riboflavin, pantothenic acid, niacin, pyridoxine, biotin, folic acid, choline and B12, and Vitamin C and ascorbic acid. B-vitamins help convert food to energy; Vitamin C can be manufactured by the dog and supplementation is not necessary. However, some breeders insist that Vitamin C is helpful for dogs that are under stress.

Fat-soluble vitamins include Vitamins A, D, E and K. They contribute to and are involved in several body functions, including eyesight, bone formation and strength, cell stability and blood coagulation.

MINERALS

Minerals are essential for bone formation, muscle metabolism, fluid balance and nervous system function. Minerals are divided into major and trace concentrations. Calcium and phosphorus are necessary in particular ratio for bone formation and strength. An imbalance in the ratio will cause bone problems. Potassium is found within tissue cells and is important in cellular activity; a deficiency causes muscle weakness and heart and

---

TYPES OF FOODS/TREATS

There are three types of commercially available dog food—dry, canned and semi-moist—and a huge assortment of treats (lucky dogs) to feed your dog. Which should you choose?

Dry and canned foods contain similar ingredients. The primary difference between them is their moisture content. The moisture is not just water; it's blood and broth, too, the very things that dogs adore. So while canned food is more palatable, dry food is more economical, convenient and effective in controlling tartar buildup. Most owners feed a 25% canned/75% dry diet to give their dogs the benefit of both. Just be sure your dog is getting the nutrition he needs (you and your veterinarian can determine this).

Semi-moist food has the flavor dogs love and the convenience owners want. However, it tends to contain excessive amounts of artificial colors and preservatives.

Dog treats come in every size, shape and flavor imaginable, from organic cookies shaped like postmen to beefy chew sticks. Dogs seem to love them all, so enjoy the variety. Just be sure not to overindulge your dog. Factor treats into his regular meal sizes.

kidney lesions. Sodium is found in fluids outside the tissue cells and performs a function similar to potassium. It is usually found in the diet as sodium chloride—salt—and is rarely deficient. Excess sodium has been linked to hypertension in dogs. Magnesium is found in soft tissue and bone; it interacts with calcium to provide proper heart, muscle and nervous tissue function and aids in metabolism of potassium and sodium.

Trace elements are iron, copper, manganese, zinc, iodine, selenium and cobalt. Although dietary requirements are minimal, they are essential to general good health. Iron is critical for healthy red blood cells and an essential component of some enzymes. Iron from animal sources appears to be more readily absorbed than that from vegetable sources. There is some evidence that feeds high in soy products could interfere with iron absorption, leading to a recommendation that soy-based foods be supplemented with a higher-than-normally-required iron supplement. Zinc contributes to skin and coat health, enzyme function and protein synthesis. Copper is necessary in production of melanin, the pigment that colors coat and skin and is linked with iron metabolism.

HOW MANY MEALS A DAY?

Individual dogs vary in how much they should eat to maintain a desired body weight—not too fat, but not too thin. Puppies need several meals a day, while older dogs may only need one. Determine how much food keeps your adult dog looking and feeling his best. Then decide how many meals you want to feed with that amount. Like us, most dogs love to eat, and offering two meals a day is more enjoyable for them. If you're worried about overfeeding, make sure you measure correctly and abstain from adding tidbits to the meals.

Whether you feed one or two meals, only leave your dog's food out for the amount of time it takes him to eat it—10 minutes, for example. Freefeeding (when food's available any time) and leisurely meals encourage picky eating. Don't worry if your dog doesn't finish all his dinner in the allotted time. He'll learn he should.

Preservatives

Preservatives are necessary in foods that contain animal fats to prevent rancidity. The fats that are used in dry kibble for palatability, a source of fatty acids, and a carrier for fat-soluble vitamins can cause dog food to become toxic if they break down. Dog food manufacturers use several chemicals called antioxidants to

prevent that breakdown, including BHA, BHT, ethoxyquin and Vitamins C and E.

Vitamins are used as preservatives in all natural and
organic foods. They are more expensive than other
chemicals and not as efficient at the job. Foods preserved with vitamins have a shorter shelf life than food
preserved with BHA, BHT and ethoxyquin.

Which Dog Food to Choose

If a dog food is balanced and provides the proper
amount of essential nutrients, which of the dozens of
brands and hundreds of formulas should be chosen
for your Maltese?

The food must contain nutrients in usable form.
Proteins, carbohydrates, vitamins and minerals are no
good if they can not be absorbed. Higher-priced diets
are more likely to have balanced and usable nutrients
than less expensive foods.

The food must be palatable to the dog. If your Maltese
does not like it, it does not matter how well balanced
it is.

Your Maltese must remain healthy while eating the
food. If his skin is dry, he is losing or gaining weight,
has stomach gas or flatulence, consider changing his
diet.

Although allergies in dogs seem to be on the increase,
few dogs are actually allergic to their food. Lamb and
rice feeds were formulated a few years ago as diets for
dogs allergic to poultry, beef or corn, but there is little
evidence that the itchy skin and malabsorption problems experienced by many dogs could actually be
traced to food allergies.

Major dog food manufacturers make every effort to provide a balanced diet of proper nutrients in usable form,
but in the end the choice of a dog food is personal,
preferably done as a result of careful consideration.

As noted earlier, a diet of foods that is high in protein
and fat content will contribute to the health of the
Maltese's long, beautiful coat.

Types of Dog Food

KIBBLE FOODS

Dry food or kibbles are made from dough of grain flours, meat meals, dairy products and vitamins and minerals baked in large pans and broken after cooking. Many kibbled foods are prepared in a mixing pressure cooker and the resulting dough is extruded

through a die and expanded with steam and air into small, porous nuggets. These nuggets are coated with a liquid fat, carbohydrate or milk product for added calories and palatability. These feeds must be at least 40 percent carbohydrates in order for the process to work and must be packaged in bags with a grease barrier of impermeable material such as plastic-coated paper.

Most experts believe that dry foods provide an excellent source of nutrition for dogs.

SEMI-MOIST FOODS

Semi-moist foods are cooked combinations of soybean meal, sugar, fresh meat or meat by-products, animal fat, preservatives and humectants (wetting agents that allow the product to stay moist but not spoil). The dough is extruded into a variety of shapes to resemble ground meat or chunks of meat to appeal to the buyer; the dog does not care about the food's appearance. The coloring in semi-moist foods can turn the dog's stool reddish. This red-colored food can cause an increased tendency for tear staining so these foods should be fed with caution to a Maltese.

CANNED FOODS

Canned foods come in four types: ration, all animal tissue, chunk-style and stew. The ration foods are ground and cooked into a liquid, then canned. The animal-tissue foods are not liquefied before canning and may include chunks of identifiable by-products such as arteries. Chunk-style foods are ground and shaped into chunks to disguise the by-products, then covered with gravy before the can is sealed. Stews are designed to please the owner. In each of these types, the filled cans are sterilized.

FROZEN DOG FOOD

Frozen dog food is available in limited distribution. This is a meat-based food with no preservatives. It generally contains a sweetener such as cane molasses that adds to the caloric content. It must be kept frozen until ready to use and the unused portion must be kept refrigerated.

Supplements

Many nutritionists and veterinarians feel that a dog being fed a balanced diet that meets his requirement for nutrients does not need any supplements of vitamins or minerals. Some go so far as to say that supplements can unbalance the diet by disrupting the necessary relationship between vitamins and minerals. Some breeders disagree and regularly supplement their dogs with one of a variety of products promoted for healthy coats and skin, bone growth or reproductive capacity.

Owners of dogs with dry skin may add a teaspoon or tablespoon of corn oil to their pet's dinner, but many nutritionists think that this adds only calories and that a food higher in essential fatty acids will take care of the skin. Some owners purchase essential fatty acids in a bottle and add that to the food.

> **TO SUPPLEMENT OR NOT TO SUPPLEMENT?**
>
> If you're feeding your dog a diet that's correct for his developmental stage and he's alert, healthy looking and neither over- nor underweight, you don't need to add supplements. These include table scraps as well as vitamins and minerals. In fact, a growing puppy is in danger of developing musculoskeletal disorders by over-supplementation. If you have any concerns about the nutritional quality of the food you're feeding, discuss them with your veterinarian.

Finally, some owners think growing puppies need extra calcium and add it in the form of bone meal. But this

49

can do more harm than good, for calcium must be in balance with phosphorus and magnesium in the diet, and an overabundance of calcium can cause a myriad of problems.

Clearly, supplementation of a dog's regular diet is controversial. Most Maltese will do well when fed good quality dry dog food; occasionally add some canned or frozen food, some meat broth (no salt added) or a bit of liver for a treat; and avoid supplements unless recommended by a veterinarian.

Those owners who would like to cook their own food at home should contact a nutritionist for a recipe to make sure the ration is balanced.

Feeding the Older Maltese

As your Maltese becomes a senior citizen his nutritional requirements may change. As he gets older he will naturally be less active than he was as a puppy and as a young adult, and therefore may need less energy from his diet. A special diet is sometimes needed for him as he grows elderly. Adjustment in the content of protein he gets might be needed as organs can become less efficient. Many of the major brands of dog food have formulas available for the elderly dog.

Obesity

Obesity in dogs is a serious medical problem. Fat dogs are more at risk in surgery, more prone to injury and have more stress on their heart, lungs, liver, kidneys and joints. Fat complicates diseases and stresses the body. Health factors associated with obesity include skeletal stress, cardiopulmonary disease, interference with normal reproductive functions and puppy delivery, complications to diabetes, difficulty in regulating body temperature and potential inflammation of the pancreas. Surgery takes longer if the veterinarian has to work his way through layers of fat, and obesity complicates drug therapy, anesthesia and recovery from injury.

Approximately 25-30 percent of dogs either suffer from obesity or are at risk of becoming obese. Dogs become obese because they take in more calories than they use. They will eat themselves into oblivion if given half a chance, so you must be on your toes.

To avoid obesity, tailor the Maltese diet to his activity level, walk the dog daily and cut back on treats, especially high fat treats. Do not depend on the dog to exercise himself in the back yard; like many people, dogs will not exercise sufficiently without some incentive to do so. A regular schedule of walks and a lower calorie diet will help avoid obesity.

To return a heavy dog to a healthy weight, work with a veterinarian to rule out hormonal problems, determine the dog's optimum weight and devise a feeding schedule that will achieve that weight with a minimum of stress on the dog. Some dog food companies have a special formula for overweight dogs that contains fewer calories. If the dog is very hungry, a diet high in moisture may do the trick because it provides more volume.

Use common sense in feeding your Maltese— to avoid obesity, don't overfeed your dog, and be sure he gets an adequate amount of exercise.

Treats

There are many commercially prepared dog biscuits that make excellent rewards and snacks. There are also preserved, packaged meat products, either beef or lamb based, that can be cut into small bites for treats. You can find these products at most stores that carry dog food. Care should be taken not to overfeed these treats, and be sure to include treats when assessing your dog's daily caloric intake.

Those interested in healthy foods will find that Maltese like vegetables such as raw carrots and broccoli cut up into little bits. Maltese seem to like the crunchy taste of these treats, which are also excellent stimulation for the gums.

Sliced beef liver and a bunch of garlic (the kind that comes cut up in a bottle) boiled until the beef liver is cooked through (30 minutes) makes an excellent homemade treat. The resultant liver is quite messy, but this problem can be solved by placing it on a baking sheet in the oven at 250°F, turning once until each side is dried out—but not dried to the point of the entire piece being hard. Cut this up into little bits and keep in refrigerator. Maltese love this treat—but you do need to use care to not give them too much as it can cause diarrhea.

An alternative to beef liver is beef hearts. Basically cook this the same way as the liver above. Ask your butcher for beef hearts or have them ordered for you. They are usually quite inexpensive. You may need to buy a whole heart but the butcher will usually cut it up for you and you can freeze until needed. When cooked this tastes much like roast beef and again the Maltese love this treat. Beef heart treats do not cause the diarrhea that comes with too many liver treats.

chapter 6

Grooming
Your
Maltese

It's difficult not to admire the elegant, flowing coat of a Maltese flying around the show ring. Many Maltese owners ask what they need to do to have a beautiful coat on their Maltese. The answer is that good coats are "bred, fed and cared for." Your Maltese was bred selectively by experienced breeders who kept in mind the traits in the Standard discussed in chapter one. The previous chapter

discussed feeding your Maltese. The final part of a beautiful coat is the grooming care your Maltese receives.

Basic Grooming Supplies

Do not underestimate the importance of using good supplies and equipment to groom your Maltese. You will need a pin brush,

GROOMING
TOOLS

pin brush

slicker brush

flea comb

towel

mat rake

grooming
glove

scissors

nail clippers

tooth-cleaning
equipment

shampoo

conditioner

clippers

comb(s), slicker brush, scissors, nail clippers, rubber bands and hair dryer. When selecting a pin brush, choose one that has good deep pins; these are needed to penetrate the Maltese coat. The most basic comb is the Belgium Greyhound comb; these combs are made of steel and glide through the hair much better and break less coat than other kinds. Greyhound combs in both a large and small size are good to have in your grooming supplies. A rat-tail parting comb from the beauty supply store is another useful comb for making the straight part down the middle of the back. A small soft slicker brush is a must, and the triangle shaped ones are particularly good for getting those difficult places like the underarms. There are several varieties of nail clippers, but the preferred type for Maltese nails is the guillotine type. Good quality scissors are needed to cut hair on the feet and around the face. The small orthodontic type of rubber bands or small barrettes are useful for holding the hair out of the face of the Maltese. A hair dryer is needed dry the coat of your Maltese following her bath.

Training to Be Groomed

Train your puppy to lay on her back and/or side and be groomed when she is young. The best time to train is when she is tired and willing to lie quietly or rest. Even though a young Maltese puppy does not require a lot of grooming, you need to train her when she is young, before her coat starts getting mats and tangles so she will accept the grooming that will become a necessary part of her life. If she gets used to it at an early age, she will be more cooperative during grooming sessions, and you will both be happier.

BRUSHING TECHNIQUES

Brushing your dog is the single most important thing that you can do to keep the coat looking nice and mat free. You must brush at least every other day if you have your dog in full coat. When brushing, continually mist the hair with a conditioner spray (for example, the conditioner used as a rinse after bathing). A tiny

bit of coat oil may be added to the conditioner. The
conditioning mist helps avoid breaking the coat.

It is important to brush the entire coat and not just the
top portions. Start with a pin brush and work your way
though the coat. Use the parting comb to separate
the hair. Start at the underside and work up to the
rest of the coat. The method that you use is important.
A common problem many peo-
ple have trying to grow a long
coat is "flipping the wrists." The
grooming stroke should be a long
stroke through the hair finished
off with the wrist flat. When one
finishes the stroke by flipping up
the wrist, microscopic pieces of
hair can break off the ends of
the coat. Over time this repeated
practice can cause a coat to discon-
tinue growing.

PARTING

Stack your Maltese on a table and
stand directly behind her. (Make
sure the dog is standing so that her spine is straight.)
Using the end tooth of a metal comb or a knitting needle and beginning at the base of the dog's neck, run
the tooth of the comb straight down the spine, allowing the coat to fall to either side.

*The grooming
stroke should be
a long stroke
through the hair
finished off with
the wrist flat.*

REMOVING MATS

If you find a mat, gently separate it with your fingertips.
Brushing through it will result in hair loss. To remove
a mat, spray it lightly with water to lubricate the hair. If
the mat you are removing is large and packed solid,
you may have to spray it with detangler or, better yet, a
coat conditioning oil until it is saturated. You and your
Maltese will both need a lot of patience. Pull the mat
apart as much as possible with your fingers; then use
the end tooth of the comb to loosen the individual
hairs. Work on the mat from whichever side allows you

the best access. Do not cut the mat out unless you want a big hole in your dog's coat and only cut through the mat as a last resort, if it is so solidly packed that you have no other choice.

To loosen the mat, you may have to use more oil or detangler as you progress, and you may have to allow it to soak for a while before it does its job. Alternate between separating the mat with your fingers and separating it with the end tooth of your comb. Never try to pull the entire mat out at once with the comb or brush. It hurts your dog and she will let you know that she does not appreciate what you are doing.

The coat should be free of all mats before you bathe your Maltese; water only serves to set mats in tighter.

Bathing

The frequency with which you will need to bathe your dog will depend upon whether or not you are showing your dog, your dog's coat type (some are more prone to matting if they are not bathed weekly) and the environment in which the dog lives (obviously a dog who goes outside often will need to be bathed more than one that doesn't). A good bathing schedule for a Maltese would be to bathe every seven to ten days. Follow the shampoo with a conditioner. Care should be used during the shampoo process. Excessive rubbing can cause breakage and matting. The best results will be achieved by pouring the shampoo and conditioner over the coat and gently cleansing.

Have everything necessary at hand—towels, shampoo and conditioner—ready before you put your Maltese in the tub. Clean your dog's ears if necessary and place a small ball of cotton in the ears to soak up any water accidentally entering the ear canal (a common cause of infection). Place a rubber mat or towel on the bottom of the sink or bathtub. A hand-held rubber spray attached to your faucet can make things much easier.

Make sure your Maltese is completely wet to the skin before applying shampoo. Apply dabs of shampoo to the back, each leg and under the tail of your dog. Work up a good lather down to the skin, proceeding from back to front. Take special care to clean the anal area and paw pads. Rinse the coat thoroughly and shampoo again. Rinse again. Wash your dog's face with a washcloth. Take great care to avoid the getting shampoo in the eyes. Tip the head up to rinse. Rinse every part of the body until all traces of soap are gone and the water runs perfectly clear.

At this point, you may add a conditioner. Allow it to stay in the coat for the time recommended by the manufacturer and then rinse from the coat. When the bath is finished, squeeze all the excess water from the ears, legs and tail before removing the dog from the tub. When towel drying your Maltese, squeeze or blot the coat with the towel to remove as much moisture as possible. Do not rub the coat with the towel as this can cause tangling and mats.

Rinse every part of the body until all traces of soap are gone.

WHICH SHAMPOOS TO USE?

It is important to choose the right shampoos and conditioners when grooming a Maltese. The pH of normal canine skin has a reported range of about 7.0 to 7.4. The neutral point on the pH scale is 7.0, therefore canine skin should be considered mildly alkaline. Human skin, in contrast, has a pH of approximately 5.5. Using products designed for humans, which are acidic, will sooner or later cause damage to your Maltese coat. There are a number of good canine products on the market. Select a shampoo that will cleanse well. Whitening shampoos may help brighten the coat of a Maltese, but long term use of these products may cause dryness of the hair and result in coat breakage. Follow the shampoo with a good cream rinse or conditioner.

BLOW DRYING

Following the bath a Maltese should be blown dry. Inexpensive stand dryers are available that work well for many people. This type of dryer will sit on a table or counter and allow the use of one hand to brush the Maltese hair and the other hand to keep your Maltese out of danger. Use only the medium heat setting of your dryer. Using high heat can cause the coat the break more readily. As you direct the heat from the dryer to the coat use a long, firm, grooming stroke. Continue with one section until it feels dry to the touch and then move on to another. Many times the feet and leg furnishings can be dried easier using a slicker brush. The face furnishings should be dried last using a small metallic comb.

Grooming Feet

The hair between the pads of the Maltese foot grows quite long and quite fast. If ignored, it tends to mat. Left alone, the mats increase in size and can spread the pads further apart.

Keeping the pads neatly trimmed is an easy task. With the dog on her side or back, hold a leg steady at an angle that is comfortable for you. The hand that holds the leg will have to do double duty because you'll need to spread the pads slightly apart to trim down between them. Some groomers use a clipper (such as a mustache trimmer) for this task, others use small scissors.

Shaggy feet make even the most neatly groomed Maltese look "unfinished." The unkempt appearance of those feet can be improved simply by trimming and rounding the coat around the feet. Push the hair up and away from the foot itself and hold it there. Brush or comb a layer of hair over the foot and trim it all the way around fairly close to the foot. Then brush a second layer over the foot, this time trimming it so that it's slightly longer than the first layer. De-pending on how heavily coated your dog's foot is, repeat this until the foot has a neat, rounded ap-pearance. Do all four feet in the same way.

TRIMMING NAILS

It is of paramount importance to clip the nails every week—just after a bath is the best time when the nails are soft. Purchase dog nail clippers at a pet sup-ply store. Nail clippers are available in two styles: "guillotine" style and scissors style. The guillotine style has replaceable blades and the scissors have a notch cut in the blade to fit the nail. Never use clippers for human nails, which can split and injure the nails. Dogs have thick nails, so be sure your clippers have sharp blades. Have stypic powder, flour or cornstarch on hand in case you accidentally nick a quick.

Clip your Maltese nails under good lighting. Most Maltese nails are white or light colored, and the

darker center of the quick is unmistakable. However, some Maltese have dark nails and the quick is not visible. In this case, clip only the ends of the nails. You may have to cut them more frequently to achieve a proper length. Cut at a perpendicular (90°) angle to the nail. Remember to also clip the nail of the dewclaws. After you clip them, filing the nails with a human or dog nail file helps to smooth the sharp edges.

Nails should be clipped on a weekly basis—right after a bath, when the nails are soft, is a good time for a trim.

Cleaning Teeth

Dogs should have their teeth brushed—every day if possible. This is especially important for older dogs that are more likely to have plaque buildup. Be sure to use toothpaste made for dogs. Toothpaste for humans contains ingredients that can upset a dog's stomach.

59

If your Maltese struggles, try wrapping her in a large towel to gently restrain her. Follow-up the brushing with praise and play, so that your Maltese associates the experience with something positive. If your dog simply refuses to have her teeth brushed, there are cleansing gels on the market containing zinc ascorbate that can be effective in controlling plaque and tartar when used daily. The gel can be sprayed or rubbed inside the dog's mouth.

Grooming Ears

Apply ear powder to the inside of each ear, making certain the hair is thoroughly covered, especially at the base. Wait a few minutes to allow the powder to dry the hair. It is surprising how much easier the hair is to pluck once the powder has dried and how much less your Maltese will mind the plucking if the powder is used.

Pluck only a few hairs at a time, because this is less irritating for the dog. You can use your fingers to pull out the majority of the hair; however, if you prefer, you may also use tweezers or a hemostat.

Tear Staining

There are several ways to remove tear staining from the facial hair. Take care not to allow these products, or any other chemical solutions, to get in your dog's eyes. It is also important to remember that when attempting to remove tear staining you may also be damaging the hair, make sure that you condition the hair before you start. Pack the facial furnishings with a good quality conditioner for several days before removing the tear staining.

Mix an equal volume of Milk of Magnesia and human hair peroxide (20 volume), and then use cornstarch to make a good paste. Apply and work well into the stained area and let dry overnight. Wash out and condition well. Keep doing this for several days until tear staining is gone, skipping a day or two between applications if possible. Do not be impatient. If you have a face that is badly stained it may take several attempts to bring the color back to white.

Yellow Stains

It is not unusual for Maltese to stain yellow on their feet from urine, mud and other things. A good formula to remove this yellow color is one made of 50 percent liquid Woolite and 50 percent human hair peroxide (20 volume), diluted 50 percent with water. Shampoo this mixture into the stained portion of the coat and let it remain for three to five minutes. Wash out and shampoo and condition as normal.

Leisure Trims for Adult Maltese

Maintaining a long, flowing coat is a lot of work. The solution is a short trim known variously as a "leisure clip," "puppy cut," "cocker clip," "Poodle clip" or "Schnauzer cut." Whatever you wish to call it, a short trim gives a Maltese freedom to play and be mischievous without the worry of coat care problems. Short trims also cut down on grooming and bathing time. Many of the show exhibitors put their Maltese in these clips when the Maltese has retired from her active show career.

The first time an owner puts their Maltese in this clip they may want to enlist the services of a professional groomer. However, it is also easy to do at home. In addition to the basic grooming supplies discussed earlier in this chapter you will also need a good set of clippers. The directions that follow are for the Oster A5 clipper, using a #10 blade and a #4 or #5 blade. Oster clippers can be purchased from many of the catalog pet suppliers and many pet stores. There are other comparable brands of clippers.

LEISURE CUT PROCEDURE

First groom your Maltese with a brush, slicker and comb until all the mats have been removed from the coat. Using the Oster clipper with the #4 or #5 blade, clip the hair of the body in a downward motion for a

*How to create a
leisure cut.*

smooth finish. Clip all of the body from the neck to the
tail including the lower chest. Do not clip the legs, tail
or head. An alternative is to leave the hair on the sides
and the lower chest a little longer.

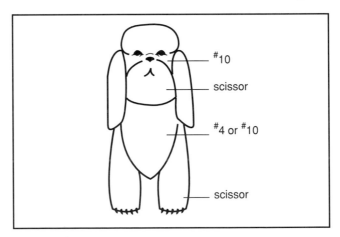

When you have finished clipping the body, you can use
your scissors to trim the legs so that the hair blends
into that of the body, leaving the hair longer toward
the feet but shorter at the top. Round off the feet to
give a nice finished look. Do not forget to trim the hair
around the pads and clip the toenails.

Next, you should work on the head and face. Using the
Oster clipper with the #10 blade, clip the hair on the
sides of the face going from the front to the back. Clip

the area under the ears short also. Leave the hair on the ears long. For the mustache and beard use your scissors and trim the area from the corner of the mouth forward into a circle. The hair above the eyes and the skull should be trimmed to about 1 - 2 inches in length so it looks as though the dog is wear-ing a lit-tle cap. Hold the hair up to cut this in a nice circle and then let it fall. As you work on the face, you may wish to initially leave the hair a little longer—with practice, you will be able to cut so that you achieve the look you desire.

Once you have completed the clipping and scissoring you should bath and blow-dry your Maltese. You may find you have missed a few straggly hairs so touch them up with your scissors.

Once in this clip, your Maltese will need to only be clipped or touched up every several months

Making top-knots: Part the hair straight back and divide into two equal sections.

Making Those Topknots

The first step in making Maltese topknots is to use a lit-tle clear gel (human hair type) in the topknot area when drying the hair to give it a bit more body. To make topknots, you will need permanent end papers or mesh, some small orthodontic rubber bands and bows. The permanent end papers or mesh should be cut into squares approximately 2 inches by 2 inches.

Have your Maltese lay her head on a small pillow while making the topknots. The pillow elevates the head and provides you with a good perspective so that you will not make the topknots too far back.

Gently tie a rubber band around each section of hair.

Start by using a rattail comb to part the hair straight back about the outside edge of each eye (approximately 1 inch above the eye). Make a part in the center and divide into two equal sections. Next, gather up the hair in each section. You may wish to back comb the section to give the hair a little more lift. Secure the section with a small rubber band. Use the rat-tail end of the comb to pull out any additional lift you desire in the front.

Next, take the end paper and fold over the top about one third. Place the fold on the top and wrap this around the rubber-banded portion of hair. Place the end paper in the back and fold each side over to the front and then wrap around to the back—the idea is to have the end paper folded in thirds.

Your Maltese will look like this with end papers and rubber bands secured.

Place the tail of the rat-tail comb behind the hair and end paper and fold the top portion over the rat-tail to give the resultant topknot a nice even fold. Then use another small rubber band to secure the topknot.

Finish the topknots by using some gel to hold down any wispy pieces of hair that are not secure in the top knot.

Finally, its time to apply the bows. Bows can be purchased from several suppliers, or you can make your own from satin ribbon. Small pieces of colored yarn also make attractive bows. Most owners prefer bows in red, royal blue, purple, green or black.

Maltese in the United States are shown with two top-knots as adults. Many puppies are shown with single topknots because they may not have enough hair to make the two topknots. In Europe and Australia, Maltese are shown with a single topknot.

Single topknots are made by gathering the hair from just above the corner of each eye and using a rat-tail comb, parting for about an inch toward the back of the dog's head. The resulting hank of hair is secured with a small rubber band. The rat-tail comb can be used in the front to get some additional lift if desired. Placing a large bow over the rubber band finishes the topknot.

Add bows. You can easily make them yourself from satin ribbon.

Choosing a Groomer

Because of the relatively elaborate techniques required to properly groom a Maltese, finding a good groomer may be a challenge. Ask your breeder and/or your veterinarian for references. Many veterinarians and boarding kennels offer grooming services. The most im-portant qualification in a Maltese groomer is experience working with coated-breed dogs. Some groomers may specialize in a certain type of dog. You do not want your Maltese to come home looking like a Terrier. Services you should reasonably expect from your groomer will include brushing out the coat, bathing (including flea dip if required), blow drying, nail trimming and filing and ear cleaning. You may want your groomer to give your Maltese a leisure clip. When you take your Maltese to the groomer be very specific in your instructions. And be realistic—if your Maltese is badly matted the groomer may have no choice but to give your dog a very short clip.

chapter 7

Keeping Your Maltese Healthy

The Maltese is basically a very healthy breed with few medical problems. You are unlikely to encounter many of the problems discussed herein, but you should be aware of them nonetheless. With good care and regular veterinary checkups you should expect your Maltese to live well into his teenage years.

Choosing a Veterinarian

Select a veterinarian that is right for you and your Maltese. Convenience and referrals from friends or your breeder may factor into your choice, but there are more technical criteria you may want to consider. Start by looking for a veterinarian who is associated with a hospital that provides the services you require. Visit the veterinary office: It should look and smell clean, and the staff should be well trained, courteous and caring. Are medical licenses to practice and hospital inspection certificates (from the American Animal Hospital Association or state veterinary association) displayed or available to you if you ask to see them? Ask for a tour of the hospital when it is mutually convenient for you and the hospital staff. Ask about the veterinarian's training and specialty areas. You may someday be in need of a referral to a specialty hospital or an after-hours emergency hospital. Does your veterinarian refer or offer to refer your pet if the problem warrants?

Vaccinations

There are three important words that you should know and understand: Vaccine, vaccination and immunity.

VACCINE

A vaccine is the liquid preparation containing the modified or killed disease-causing agent. A vaccine stimulates the dog's immune system to protect itself against disease. When the antigen or infectious agent enters the dog's body, it is recognized as foreign and antibodies are produced to bind to it and destroy it. Broadly, there are two types of vaccine—modified-live and killed. The former generally provide a stronger, longer-lasting and more rapid protection. Killed vaccines generally require a great number of, and more frequent, injections.

VACCINATION

A vaccination is the act of administering the vaccine. In animals, vaccination is usually done by injection.

> **YOUR PUPPY'S VACCINES**
>
> Vaccines are given to prevent your dog from getting an infectious disease like canine distemper or rabies. Vaccines are the ultimate preventive medicine; they're given before your dog ever gets the disease so as to protect him from the disease. That's why it is necessary for your dog to be vaccinated routinely. Puppy vaccines start at 8 weeks of age for the five-in-one DHLPP vaccine and are given every three to four weeks until the puppy is 16 months old. Your veterinarian will put your puppy on a proper schedule and will re-mind you when to bring in your dog for shots.

IMMUNITY

Immunity is the effect of vaccination, protection from disease. Vaccination "tricks" the immune system into

*Newborn pup-
pies receive pro-
tection from
antibodies in
the mother's
milk.*

behaving as if a natural infection were occurring. Newly produced antibodies intercept disease-causing forms of the virus or bacteria. The level of immunity is influenced by several factors such as disease and stress, however, it is rare that a vaccinated animal will not develop immunity to diseases.

How Many Shots Does Your Maltese Need?

Animals, like people, are most susceptible to infectious agents during the first month of life. Newborn animals usually receive protection from antibodies in the mother's milk. To be sure that nursing animals receive this protection, the mother should be immunized before breeding. To maintain and strengthen disease resistance after the antibodies in the mother's milk have been depleted, a series of vaccinations should be administered to young animals from approximately 6 weeks to 6 months of age. Lifetime protection is maintained by annual booster vaccinations. There are many effective vaccination schedules and your Maltese is never too old to start a vaccination program. Vaccines are administered under the skin (subcutaneously), in the muscle (intramuscular), or by nasal spray.

There is no one answer to "how many shots your Maltese needs," but a few basic rules apply. A minimum of two vaccinations (including distemper and parvo) given three to four weeks apart are required for every dog or puppy over 3 months old. An additional vaccination against rabies is also necessary. Vaccinations against coronavirus, Bordatella or Lyme disease are based on owner's needs and veterinarian's advice.

For young puppies, vaccinations usually start at 6 to 8 weeks of age and are given every three to four weeks until the puppy is 16 weeks of age. Be sure to obtain a history of your puppy's vaccinations from your breeder. Bring this history with you when you visit your veterinarian. He or she will work with you to arrange a vaccination schedule for your dog.

DISEASES PREVENTED BY VACCINATIONS

Canine Distemper

Canine distemper is a highly contagious viral disease transmitted by direct or indirect contact with the discharges from an infected dog's eyes and nose. A healthy dog does not need to come in direct contact with another infected dog to contract canine distemper, because air currents and inanimate objects can carry the virus.

Early signs of canine distemper are similar to those of a severe cold and often go unrecognized by the pet owner. Vomiting and diarrhea may accompany the respiratory problems. A nervous system disorder may also develop. The death rate from canine distemper is greater than 50 percent in adult dogs and much higher in puppies. Even if the dog survives, distemper can cause permanent damage to a dog's nervous system, sense of smell, hearing and sight. Partial or total paralysis is not uncommon.

Canine Parvovirus

Parvovirus is a highly resistant virus that can withstand extreme temperature changes. Dog feces is usually the source of the infection, which can contaminate cages, shoes, and can be carried on the feet and hair of infected animals.

This virus attacks the intestinal tract, white blood cells and heart muscle. Clinical signs include vomiting, severe diarrhea accompanied by a loss of appetite, depression and high fever. Most deaths occur within 48 to 72 hours after the onset of clinical signs. Puppies less than 3 months of age can experience an inflammation of the heart (myocarditis). Infected pups may act depressed, collapse gasping for breath, and death may follow immediately. Puppies that survive are likely to have permanently damaged hearts.

Canine Parainfluenza

A virus that produces a mild respiratory tract infection causes canine parainfluenza. It is often associated with other respiratory tract viruses. In combination, these viruses are usually transmitted by contact with the nasal secretions of infected dogs. The vaccine to protect against this disease may be combined with other vaccines to offer broader protection.

Infectious Canine Hepatitis

A virus that can infect many tissues, but usually attacks the liver, causes infectious canine hepatitis. In some cases, a whiteness or cloudiness of the eye may accompany the disease. Another strain of the same virus can cause respiratory tract infections. These viruses are transmitted by contact with objects that have been contaminated with the urine from infected dogs. Infectious canine hepatitis is caused by a different virus than is human hepatitis. You cannot give hepatitis to your dog and your dog cannot give it to you.

Canine Leptospirosis

Canine leptospirosis is a bacterial disease that impairs renal (kidney) function and may result in kidney failure. Clinical signs include vomiting, impaired vision, and convulsions. The disease is transmitted by contact with the urine of infected animals or by contact with objects that have been contaminated with the urine of infected animals.

CAUTION: The immune systems of many Maltese puppies cannot tolerate the traditional vaccination against leptospirosis. Most Maltese owners will not have their veterinarians vaccinate for leptospirosis before their Maltese is one year of age.

Canine Coronavirus

Canine coronavirus is a contagious intestinal disease much like parvovirus that causes vomiting and diarrhea in dogs of all ages. Coronavirus antigens have recently been added to most vaccines to insure this extra protection.

Rabies

Rabies is a viral disease that can be contracted by any warm-blooded animal, including humans. Once infected, the disease is fatal. In most parts of the United States both dog and cat owners are legally required to have their pets vaccinated against rabies. Rabies primarily attacks the nervous system and causes encephalitis. The virus is transmitted in saliva from the bite of an infected animal. The incubation period prior to clinical signs is extremely variable, but is usually two to eight weeks. The virus will begin shedding in saliva a short time (usually less than ten days), before clinical signs develop. The primary source of rabies is the bite of a rabid wild animal. The most common of these are skunk, raccoon, bat and fox. Once clinical signs develop, there is no treatment.

There are two types of rabies, dumb and furious. Both cause a departure from normal behavior. Immediately prior to death, animals with furious rabies will have a period where they appear to be "mad," frothing at the mouth and biting anything that gets in their way. Dumb rabies differs in that there is no "mad" period.

> ### WHEN TO CALL THE VET
>
> In any emergency situation, you should call your veterinarian immediately. You can make the difference in your dog's life by staying as calm as possible when you call and by giving the doctor or the assistant as much information as possible before you leave for the clinic. That way, the vet will be able to take immediate, specific action to remedy your dog's situation.
>
> Emergencies include acute abdominal pain, suspected poisoning, snakebite, burns, frostbite, shock, dehydration, abnormal vomiting or bleeding, and deep wounds. You are the best judge of your dog's health, as you live with and observe him every day. Don't hesitate to call your veterinarian if you suspect trouble.

With dumb rabies, paralysis, usually of the lower jaw, is the first sign of the disease. The paralysis spreads to limbs and vital organs and death quickly follows.

Rabies is dangerous, deadly, but almost totally preventable by vaccination. Maltese should have an initial rabies vaccination when they are 3 to 4 months of age. The duration of protection varies from 1 to 3 years. Regular booster vaccinations are required. It is essential for your health, the health of your pet and the health of your family and neighbors that your pet's rabies vaccination be kept up-to-date.

Run your hands regularly over your dog to feel for any injuries.

Kennel Cough

The bacterium *Bordetella bronchiseptica* is a primary cause of a severe, chronic cough, tracheobronchitis, or kennel cough. In addition to the cough, some dogs develop a purulent nasal discharge. Transmission most frequently occurs by contact with the nasal secretions of infected dogs.

Vaccination is usually accomplished by the use of nasal spray. There are several effective schedules and methods for administering the vaccine. Your veterinarian will establish a schedule that is best for your dog. Make sure your Maltese has been vaccinated against *Bordetella* before being boarded at a kennel.

Internal Parasites

Dogs are victims of several internal parasites frequently referred to as worms. The most common are the roundworms that infest most puppies at some time in their young lives and tapeworms that can be a big problem when flea infestations are high. Evidence of roundworms and tapeworms can be seen without the aid of a microscope, but other worms are not so easily diagnosed. Occasionally adult whipworms can be seen in the stool when the infestation has already caused some debilitation or weight loss in the dog.

Early diagnosis of the presence and species of intestinal parasite is important, for not all worms respond to the same treatment. Stool samples should be taken to the veterinarian for microscopic examination if worms are suspected. Many veterinarians include the stool check as part of the annual health examination.

Most worm infestations cause any or all of these symptoms: diarrhea, perhaps with blood in the stool; weight loss; dry hair; general poor appearance; and vomiting, perhaps with worms in the vomitus. However, some infestations cause few or no symptoms. In fact, some worm eggs or larvae can be dormant in the dog's body and activated only in times of stress, or in the case of roundworms, until the latter stages of pregnancy, when they activate and infest the soon-to-be-born puppies.

TAPEWORMS

The tapeworm is transmitted to dogs who ingest fleas or who hunt and eat wildlife infested with tapeworms or fleas. The dog sheds segments of the tapeworm containing the eggs in its feces. These segments are flat and move about shortly after excretion. They look like grains of rice when dried and can be found either in the dog's stool or stuck to the hair around his anus. The typical over-the-counter wormer cannot kill tapeworms; see the veterinarian for appropriate treatment.

Common internal parasites (l-r): roundworm, whipworm, tapeworm and hookworm.

ROUNDWORMS

Roundworms are active in the intestines of puppies, often causing a pot-bellied appearance and poor growth. The worms may be seen in vomit or stool; a severe infestation can cause death by intestinal blockage. This worm can grow to seven inches in length. The worm eggs are protected by a hard shell and can exist in the soil for years. Dogs become infected by ingesting worm eggs from contaminated soil. The eggs hatch in the intestine and the resulting larvae, are carried to the lungs by the bloodstream. The larvae, then crawl up the windpipe and gets swallowed, often causing the pup to cough or gag. Once the larvae return to the intestine, they grow into adults. Roundworms do not typically infest adults. However, as mentioned above, the larvae can encyst in body tissue of adult bitches and activate during the last stages of pregnancy to infest puppies. Worming the bitch has no effect on the encysted larvae and cannot prevent the worms from infecting the puppies. Although roundworms can be treated with an over-the-counter wormer found in pet stores, a veterinarian is the best source of information and medication to deal with intestinal parasites. Dewormers are poisonous to the worms and can make the dog sick, especially if not used in proper dosage.

HOOKWORMS

Hookworms are small, thin worms that fasten to the wall of the small intestine and suck blood. Dogs get hookworm if they come in contact with the larvae in contaminated soil. As with roundworms, the hookworm larvae become adults in the intestine. A severe hookworm infestation can kill puppies, but chronic hookworm infection is usually not a problem in the older dog. When it does occur, the signs include diarrhea, weight loss, anemia and progressive weakness. If you suspect that your dog has contracted hookworms, he should be taken to the veterinarian, along with a stool sample for proper diagnosis and treatment.

WHIPWORMS

Adult whipworms look like pieces of thread with one enlarged end. They live in the cecum, the first section of the dog's large intestine. Infestations are usually light, so an examination of feces may not reveal the presence of eggs. Several analyses by a veterinarian may be necessary before a definitive diagnosis can be made.

PREVENTION

Roundworms that infect dogs can also infect humans, but this is an extremely rare event. Nonetheless, treatment and eradication of the worms in the environment are important. Remove dog feces from backyards every day, use appropriate vermicides under veterinary supervision, and have the dog's feces checked frequently in persistent cases. When walking your Maltese in a neighborhood or park, remove all feces so that the dog does not contribute to contamination of soil away from home as well. Dogs that are in generally good condition are not likely to contract worms, but you want to take appropriate precautions.

HEARTWORMS

Heartworm, as the name suggests, causes cardiac disease in dogs. The heartworm goes through several life stages before emergence as an adult and needs at least two hosts to complete the cycle. The mosquito serves as the host for the larval stage of the worm. The mosquito ingests the larvae when it bites an infected dog and deposits its cargo in an uninfected dog when seeking another blood meal. The larvae burrow into the dog, and for three or four months, undergo several changes to reach adult form. They then travel to the right side of the heart through a vein and await the opportunity to reproduce. Adult heartworms can reach 12 inches in length and can remain in the dog's heart for several years.

Dogs that are in good health are unlikely to contract worms when out walking, but you should take appropriate precautions.

The first sign of heartworm infestation may not manifest for a year after infection, and even then the owner may dismiss the soft cough that increases with exercise as unimportant. But the cough worsens and the dog may actually faint from exertion; he tires easily, is weak and listless, loses weight and condition, and may cough up blood. Breathing becomes more difficult as the disease progresses. The progression is traumatic: The dog's quality of life diminishes drastically and he can no longer retrieve a Frisbee or take a long walk in the park without respiratory distress. Congestive heart failure ensues, and the once-active, outgoing pet is in grave danger.

If a blood test or the onset of symptoms alert owner and veterinarian to the presence of this devastating parasite, treatment is possible and successful if the disease has not progressed too far. Even if the dog, the owner, and the owner's pocketbook survive the treatment, the dog can be re-infected the next time a mosquito bites. So, before mosquito season starts, owners should have their dogs tested for heartworm and placed on preventive. Most veterinarians use two tests before declaring a dog free of heartworm; the first test checks for larvae in the blood and the second, done with the same sample, checks for adult worms in the heart that can be present even without the larvae in the blood. Heartworm prevention costs money and requires commitment: Blood must be drawn to examine for signs of infestation before the preventive drug can be given, and the drug must be administered regularly. But the effort and the money are well spent to keep a Maltese from the discomfort and debilitation of the infliction.

Preventive drugs are only available from a veterinarian.

External Parasites

FLEAS

Fleas are found throughout the United States and are most likely to be encountered on a Maltese or in their pet bedding.

Adult fleas are small, brownish insects flattened from side to side, without wings but with powerful jumping legs. Adults can live for several years and go without feeding for months at a time under extreme conditions. Fleas can remain in a structure long after the host mammals have been removed—the dog flea re-mains on the host only long enough to feed.

The flea is a die-hard pest.

Outdoors, fleas are most abundant during humid, rainy summers. Indoors, warmth and high relative humidity are conducive to large populations of fleas. The sudden appearance of large numbers of adult fleas in mid-summer and fall ("flea seasons") is due in large part to the onset of higher humidity and temperatures, which permit larval development to accelerate.

Flea bites vary in effect from short-lived itching welts to an overall rash to symptoms which may last over a year, depend-ing on the sensitivity of the victim. Commonly, a small red spot appears where the skin has been pierced. Little swelling ensues, but the spot is accompanied by a red halo of irritated skin, which usually lasts for several hours to a day. Even if the fleas are not actually seen, their existence can be confirmed by small black specks in the coat. These are the flea feces—when a dog is bathed, they dissolve, making the water a rusty red.

To eradicate fleas altogether, you must rid your dog, your home and your yard of fleas. The flea lives outside and hops on the dog not only for travel purposes but also for nutrition. Dogs bring the fleas inside, where they lay eggs in the carpeting and furniture—anywhere your dog goes in the house. Consequently, real control is a matter of not only treating the dog but also the other environments that the flea inhabits. The yard can be sprayed, and in the house,

FIGHTING FLEAS

Remember, the fleas you see on your dog are only part of the problem—the smallest part! To rid your dog and home of fleas, you need to treat your dog *and* your home. Here's how:

• Identify where your pet(s) sleep. These are "hot spots."

• Clean your pets' bedding regularly by vacuuming and washing.

• Spray "hot spots" with a non-toxic, long-lasting flea larvicide.

• Treat outdoor "hot spots" with insecticide.

• Kill eggs on pets with a product containing insect growth regulators (IGRs).

• Kill fleas on pets per your veterinarian's recommendation.

sprays and flea bombs can be used, but there are more choices for the dog. Flea sprays are effective for one to two weeks depending on their ingredients. Dips applied to the dog's coat following a bath have equal periods of effectiveness. The disadvantage to both of these is that some dogs may respond poorly to the chemicals.

Flea collars are not particularly effective, but they do prevent the fleas from traveling to the dog's head, where it is moister and more hospitable. Some dogs may be intolerant of flea collars and children should never be allowed to handle them. Some owners opt for a product that works from the inside out. Veterinarians can apply a chemical to a spot on your dog's coat which is absorbed into the dog's body and works for up to a month to repel fleas. Another option is a pill (prescribed by a veterinarian), that you give to the dog on a regular basis in his food. The chemicals in the pill course through the dog's bloodstream, and when a flea bites, the blood kills the flea. Be aware that one type of chemical flea control often precludes the use of an-other. The directions and precautions should always be checked prior to use.

Grooming a dog thoroughly every day with a flea comb works wonders. Getting a fine-toothed flea comb through a Maltese coat can be a challenge, but its a great way to keep your dog both healthy and looking beautiful.

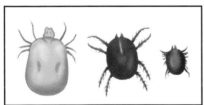

Three types of ticks (l-r): the wood tick, brown dog tick and deer tick.

TICKS

When you are grooming your Maltese, check for ticks that may have lodged in his skin, particularly around the ears or in the hair at the base of the ear, the armpits or around the genitals. If you find a tick, which is a small insect about the size of a pencil eraser when engorged with blood, smear it thoroughly with petroleum jelly. As the tick suffocates, it will back out and you can then grab it with tweezers and kill it. If the tick doesn't back out, grab it with tweezers and slowly pull it out, twist-ing very gently. Don't just grab and pull or the tick's head may separate from the body. If the head remains in the skin, an infection or abscess may result and veterinary treatment may be required.

A word of caution: Don't use your fin-gers or fingernails to pull out ticks. Ticks can carry a number of diseases, including Lyme disease, Rocky Moun-tain spotted fever and others, all of which can be very serious.

Routine Maintenance

TEAR STAINING

Many veterinary eye specialists be-lieve the actual cause of staining is excess tearing. When the face hair is wet from excess tearing it is the breeding ground for bacteria and yeast. One of the most common yeast infections is Ptyrosporin or red yeast

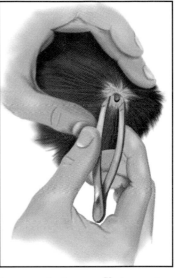

Use tweezers to remove ticks from your dog.

that causes a deep reddish-brown stain. Low-grade bac-terial infections in the tear ducts are also common and may cause excess tearing and staining. If you have a Maltese with excessive tear stains and tearing, a visit to your veterinarian may be needed. It is not unusual to find that your Maltese may have completely clogged tear ducts that need to be irrigated by your vet. As many as 20 percent of small dogs, such as Maltese, may be born with lower tear ducts that are physically closed. These tear ducts may need to be surgically opened.

Many veterinary eye specialists believe that the actual structure around the eye area plays a significant role in ex-cessive tearing. There is also genetic predisposition toward tear staining, and selective breeding can help to diminish tear staining in Maltese.

From 5 to 8 months of age, the head structure and mouth of the Maltese are undergoing many changes causing pressure on the tear ducts. Many Maltese

*Many experts
believe that the
structure of the
dog's eyes con-
tributes to exces-
sive tearing.*

puppies that have had no previous tear stain problems
will develop them during this time. It's most important
to keep the facial hair as dry as possible and frequently
wash it to help keep yeast and bacteria under control.
Make sure your Maltese has plenty of chew toys to help
relieve the pressure on the mouth during this time.

Eliminating excess tearing is one of the best ways to
stop staining. Maltese owners should pay attention to
the hair around the face and prevent hair from falling into the eyes causing irritation and infection.
Maltese can also be susceptible to allergies, and the
environment can have a negative impact on your dog's
health and appearance. It is not unusual for a Maltese

that previously had sparkling
white faces to become tear
stained overnight when in a
hotel room with someone who
smokes. It also is important to
be extra careful when bathing
your Maltese. Shampoo and
other chemicals in the eyes
can cause irritation and excess
tearing. Use a little mineral oil
to protect your Maltese's eyes
when you bathe him. You can
find this eye care product for
humans in most drug stores.

The water in many areas has a
high mineral level. If your
Maltese drinks from a water
dish and your local water has a
high mineral content you may
find the entire face and beard

stained. Training your Maltese to drink from a water
bottle can eliminate this problem. This also keeps the
face dry. Alternatively, a Maltese can be placed on puri-
fied or commercial bottled water.

Diet can play a significant key role in tear staining.
Feeding a dry kibble that is natural with no additives,
preservatives or food color in it seems to aid in maintaining white stain-free faces.

Tear staining can also be caused by fleas. The directions on most flea shampoos suggest starting the shampoo with the head. Why—because fleas need moisture to survive and get this from the dog's tears/eyes. Naturally, the fleas irritate the eyes.

Many times a rampant ear infection can be the cause of excessive tearing and staining. Your veterinarian can prescribe a good product to help alleviate ear problems. You can help by carefully drying your Maltese ears after a bath. Scraggly hairs in the ears should also be removed.

Care of the Teeth and Gums

Home care should include daily (or at least weekly) brushing, use of enzymatic "pet" toothpaste, and plaque-controlling mouth rinses. Baking soda and salt are not recommended due to their high sodium content that can contribute to heart problems. Some pet toothpaste is flavored and Maltese seem to especially like these flavor-enhanced toothpastes.

Taking an active role in the care of your dog's teeth will help reduce dental disease, bad breath (which is a symptom of dental disease), and potential life-threatening heart and kidney disease. The act of chewing hard foods and chew toys will also prevent the build up of plaque and calculus. Nylon chew toys, rawhide and hard biscuits have been shown to decrease calculus in dogs as well. The pet that eats soft food and refuses chew toys needs to have more dental care by a veterinarian and more home care by the pet owner.

Check your dog's teeth frequently and brush them regularly.

The physical process of brushing the teeth is a logical first step but requires knowledge of several basic principles to be properly accomplished. First, choose an appropriate toothbrush for your dog's mouth. Most dogs accept the act of brushing the teeth if the technique is approached in a gentle manner. It is best to start dental care with your Maltese when he is young because you want your dog to be comfortable providing access to his mouth. It is important not to try and force the mouth open. The lips should be gently parted and the brush placed on the teeth at a 45-degree angle to the long axis of the tooth. The bristles should be placed at the gum margin, establishing an angle of 45 degrees to the long axis of the tooth. Use a gentle vibratory pressure exerted up and down. The brush should be activated with a short back-and-forth motion without dislodging the tips of the bristles. Ten such strokes should be completed in the same position. The brush should then be lifted and moved to a new position and the process repeated. This cleans the teeth and avoids aggressive "scrubbing" actions. The process should be continued, section by section, covering three or four teeth at a time until all teeth are done.

You may also, on occasion, wish to have your dog's teeth cleaned professionally. Your Maltese will be anesthetized for this procedure. Some recommend frequent professional cleanings, but this is a subject that you should discuss with your veterinarian.

Retained Puppy Teeth

Maltese will typically loose their puppy teeth and cut adult teeth between 5 and 8 months of age. It is important to regularly check the mouth of your Maltese during this period of time. Many Maltese have puppy teeth with extremely long roots—especially the canines—that will not fall out naturally. If this is the case it is important that your veterinarian pull these teeth to prevent a malocclusion. Many times pulling these retained puppy teeth can be combined with a spay and neutering procedure.

Inherited Disorders
Portosystemic Shunt

Portosystemic shunt is a congenital problem that can be seen in some Maltese. During gestation the placenta delivers blood with food and oxygen from the mother through the umbilical vein. In order to make this work, there is a shunt from the liver venous circulation to the arterial circulation. At birth, the pressure within the circulatory system changes as respiration occurs and this closes the shunt, which eventually disappears. If this reverse in circulation does not occur, the liver is deprived of a blood supply and does not develop properly after birth. Many puppies can live with the small functioning portion of the liver for some time but eventually have problems and usually die if the situation is uncorrected.

Most shunts cause recognizable clinical signs by the time a dog is a young adult. Because the severity of the condition can vary widely depending on how much blood flow is diverted past the liver, it is possible for a lot of variation in clinical signs and time of onset of signs to occur. Often, this condition is recognized after a puppy fails to grow, making an early diagnosis pretty common.

Signs of portosystemic shunts include poor weight gain, sensitivity to sedatives (especially diazepam), depression, head pressing (pushing the head against a solid object), seizures, weakness, salivation, vomiting, poor appetite, increased drinking and urinating, balance problems and frequent urinary tract disease or early onset of bladder stones. If the signs of problems increase dramatically after eating, this is a strong supportive sign of a portosystemic shunt.

This malady can be diagnosed by a veterinarian but there is no simple procedure to do so. If portosystemic shunt is found, a low protein diet, which decreases the amount of ammonia produced by the dog, will be recommended. In almost all cases, surgery is recommended. There are risks with such a surgery and the recovery must be in intensive care. A Maltese owner faced with portosystemic shunt should see a board-certified veterinary surgeon to discuss the procedure at length.

LUXATED PATELLA

Luxated patellas or "slipped stifles" are a common orthopedic problem in small dogs, and female dogs are 1.5 times more likely to be affected than males.

Patellar luxation is a dislocation of the kneecap (patella). It may result from injury or congenital (present at birth) deformities.

The crippling effects of patellar luxation are related to the severity and duration of the luxation. The milder forms, especially in small breeds, show little or no signs, and only minimal treatment is required. Severe cases cause more intense pain, with limping.

Treatment ranges from rest (decreasing your pet's activity for one to two weeks) to surgical reconstruction of the knee joint. Treatment is based upon the severity of signs and your pet's age, breed and weight (obesity complicates surgery and convalescence). A weight-reduction program may be required in conjunction with treatment. Satisfactory results are usually obtained if the joint degeneration has not progressed too far. Once the condition is repaired, most affected Maltese will make a satisfactory recovery.

COLLAPSING TRACHEA

When the trachea collapses, air can no longer move freely through it. Then the animal breathes with difficulty and exhibits a honking cough.

Causes include trauma to the windpipe, nerve damage, inherited tracheal weakness, degeneration of cartilage and abnormal airflow in and out of the lungs. This con-dition is commonly found in small breeds of dogs in-cluding Maltese, and closely resembles kennel cough.

If your Maltese has any of the symptoms of collapsing trachea your should visit your veterinarian. He should perform a complete physical examination. X-rays are often necessary to confirm a diagnosis of tracheal collapse. Depending on the severity of the condition, treatment may include surgery and/or medical therapy. In mild cases, a change in lifestyle of your Maltese may be all that is necessary. Some cases of collapsing trachea cannot be cured, and treatment is directed at decreasing the severity and frequency of breathing difficulties.

White shaker dog syndrome is not a very scientific name, but it describes the condition exactly. Small white dogs such as Maltese can develop severe tremors for unexplained reasons. These dogs usually have bizarre eye movements that get much worse when excited or stressed. The usual treatment for this is to give diazepam to control the tremors and prednisone to control the symptoms. Veterinarians do not yet know the cause of this syndrome.

Spaying and Neutering

There are many myths about canine reproductive needs. Chiefly among these are the suspicion that neutering turns a male into a sissy and spaying causes a female to get fat and to lament her lost capacity.

The truth is that male dogs are better pets if they are neutered. They have less desire to roam, to mark territory, or to exert dominance over family members. They are also healthier pets: No testicles means no testicular cancer, which is not uncommon among aging intact male dogs.

Females are also better pets if they do not experience estrus twice each year. Heat cycles bring hormonal changes that can lead to personality changes. Repeated heat cycles subject the reproductive system to uterine and mammary cancers and uterine infections. Some bitches experience false pregnancies that can be an annoyance.

ADVANTAGES OF SPAY/NEUTER

The greatest advantage of spaying (for females) or neutering (for males) your dog is that you are guaranteed your dog will not produce puppies. There are too many puppies already available for too few homes. There are other advantages as well.

ADVANTAGES OF SPAYING

No messy heats.

No "suitors" howling at your windows or waiting in your yard.

Decreased incidences of pyometra (disease of the uterus) and breast cancer.

ADVANTAGES OF NEUTERING

Lessens male aggressive and territorial behaviors, but doesn't affect the dog's personality. Behaviors are often owner-induced, so neutering is not the only answer, but it is a good start.

Prevents the need to roam in search of bitches in season.

Decreased incidences of urogenital diseases.

Maltese do not get fat simply as a result of sterilization surgery. They gain weight if they eat too much and exercise too little.

Maltese owners who decide not to spay their females and neuter their males bear a responsibility to prevent their intact pets from adding to the population of pets that wind up in animal shelters. If there is a pregnancy, provide the best nutrition and veterinary care for the bitch and the puppies and carefully place the pups in good homes. Be prepared to deal with a problem pregnancy or delivery, to provide training and behavior information to puppy buyers, and to take back or help place any puppy that doesn't work in his original home.

Emergency First Aid

Dog owners can treat minor injuries and medical conditions for their pets if they have the appropriate remedies, tools and equipment available. A home first aid kit should include the following items: Cotton gauze bandage wrap—1 inch width and 2 inch width, vet wrap—2 inch width, and 4 inch width (4 inch is sold for horses), Ace bandage, first aid tape, cotton gauze pads, regular Band-Aids, cotton swabs, Benadryl, ascriptin (buffered aspirin), Pepto Bismol tablets, New Skin liquid bandage (useful for patching abrasions on pads), iodine tablets (if you hike and camp in areas where the stream water may not be safe for consumption without first treating with iodine or boiling), oral syringes (for administering liquid oral

A FIRST-AID KIT

Keep a canine first-aid kit on hand for general care and emergencies. Check it periodically to make sure liquids haven't spilled or dried up, and replace medications and materials after they're used. Your kit should include:

Activated charcoal tablets

Adhesive tape
(1 and 2 inches wide)

Antibacterial ointment
(for skin and eyes)

Aspirin (buffered or enteric coated, *not* Ibuprofen)

Bandages: Gauze rolls (1 and 2 inches wide) and dressing pads

Cotton balls

Diarrhea medicine

Dosing syringe

Hydrogen peroxide (3%)

Petroleum jelly

Rectal thermometer

Rubber gloves

Rubbing alcohol

Scissors

Tourniquet

Towel

Tweezers

medicines, getting ear-drying solution into ears, and the like...very useful!), needle and thread, safety pins in several sizes, razor blade (paper wrapped for protection), matches, tweezers, hemostat (useful for pulling ticks, thorns and large splinters), small blunt end scissors, canine rectal thermometer (get one made specifically for dogs), antibiotic ointment (such as Bacitracin, Betadine, or others), eye rinsing solution (simple mild eye wash), small bottle of 3% hydrogen peroxide, small bottle of isopropyl alcohol (rubbing), alcohol or antiseptic wipes (in small individual packets), small jar of petroleum jelly and specific medications *your* dog may need (for allergies, seizures, etc.).

If your dog has severe allergies to bee stings or other things that might be commonly encountered in places you take your dog, consider asking your veterinarian about stocking your first aid kit with medication that might be needed for that sort of special emergency. Be sure to clearly *label* all medications and supplies with their name and expiration date. Be sure to replace medications that may have exceeded their recommended expiration date. Go through your kit at least once a year to replace expired medications and replenish used supplies.

Use a scarf or old hose to make a temporary muzzle, as shown.

MUZZLING FOR SAFETY

Any dog that is injured or frightened may bite. For an emergency muzzle use a cord, necktie, piece of gauze or leash. The muzzle should be snug but not so tight as to cause discomfort or interfere with circulation. Remove as soon as possible be-cause dogs perspire through their tongues.

87

CHOKING

If your dog is choking, wrap him in a heavy blanket to keep him still. Remove the foreign object with pliers or fingers. Do not pull on a thread or string as there may be a needle attached; get veterinary help.

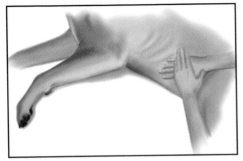

Applying abdominal thrusts can save a choking dog.

HEATSTROKE

Never leave your dog unattended in direct sunlight or in a closed vehicle in warm weather. In a car, heat can build up to an intolerable level in minutes causing brain damage or even death. Signs of heatstroke are panting, drooling, rapid pulse, fever and shock. Immediately immerse the dog in cool water (or use a hose) to lower the body temperature to normal (101.5°F). Do not lower the temperature below this level. If the dog is conscious, encourage him to drink water in small amounts to replace body fluids.

Make a temporary splint by wrapping the leg in firm casing, then bandaging it.

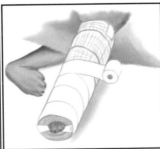

EXTERNAL WOUNDS

Small wounds should be cleaned with soap and water. Then apply an antiseptic and bandage to the wound. When possible bring the edges of the wound together and hold them in this position with adhesive tape. If an artery has been severed, bright red blood will spurt from the wound with each heartbeat. If this is the case, and the wound is in on extremity, place a tourniquet on the affected limb between the wound and the heart.

Loosen this every 15 minutes and reapply. Blood from a vein will be much darker in color and can usually be controlled with a pressure bandage. In either case seek veterinary help as soon as possible.

BURNS

For thermal (heat) burns first apply cold water or an ice pack for 20-30 minutes; follow this with an antibiotic ointment. For caustic burns such as those from chemicals, apply vinegar followed by an antibiotic preparation. For acid burns, apply a paste of bicarbonate of soda (baking soda). Electrical burns usually produce extensive tissue damage and fluid in the lungs. If the Maltese is unconscious and not breathing give artificial respiration and get veterinary help as soon as possible.

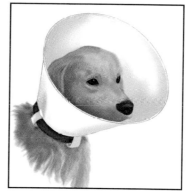

An Elizabethan collar keeps your dog from licking a fresh wound.

CARDIAC ARREST

Lay your Maltese on his right side. Flex the left elbow and press firmly at this site (where the elbow meets the body) with the palm of your hand. Repeat at a rate of sixty to eighty compressions per minutes. Cardiac massage should be combined with artificial respiration (blowing into the nostrils with the mouth closed). Try to continue compressions while giving artificial respiration. To take the pulse of your Maltese, press the middle and index fingers against the inside of your dog's hind leg, just below where it joins the body.

RESPIRATORY ARREST

If your Maltese has stopped breathing, place him on his right side with his head and neck extended. Gently draw the tongue forward and clear any objects from the mouth and throat. Place a hand on the ribs immediately behind the shoulder blades and use a sudden but gentle downward movement. Then, immediately release the pressure. This should be repeated at five-second intervals. Be careful—a distressed Maltese can bite.

SHOCK

Shock can follow almost any type of injury. Signs include shallow breathing, pale, gray-colored mucous membranes, glassy eyes, dilated pupils and collapse. Keep your Maltese warm and quiet. Immediate veterinary help should be sought as soon as possible.

*Squeeze eye oint-
ment into the
lower lid.*

EYE IRRITATIONS

If you suspect there is something in the eye of your Maltese, inspect it gently by parting the lids under a bright light. Rinse the surface of the eye and lids with plain water using an eyedropper or by squeezing a cotton ball so it drips. Do not rub. If you can see the object, gently remove it with cotton.

Giving Your Maltese Medicines

Liquids: With the head of your Maltese angled upward, pull out the bottom lip at the side of the muzzle to form a pouch and pour the medicine slowly—if you pour too quickly, the dog may choke. Using a syringe is often easier than a spoon.

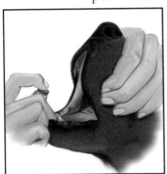

*To give a pill,
open the mouth
wide, then drop
it in the back of
the throat.*

Pills: First place one hand over the upper jaw of your Maltese, and with your thumb and fingers on either side, open the mouth by pressing gently. With the other hand pull down the lower jaw, then place the pill well back on the tongue. Close the jaws, lift the head slightly and wait for the dog to swallow—stroking the throat may help speed the process. If this does not work you can also place the pill in a small piece of meat or cheese. Just make sure the dog does not eat the treat and spit out the pill.

Poisoning

Chocolate, anti-freeze, and pesticides are some of the common household materials that can cause severe reactions and death in Maltese. House plants such as aloe vera, dieffenbachia, draecena, asparagus fern, rubber plant, schefflera, and poinsettia and outdoor favorites including azalea, rhododendron, hibiscus, and lily of the valley are among dozens of plants that can cause a variety of negative reactions in dogs. Apple seeds and cherry pits can also poison a Maltese. Some signs of plant poisoning are continual vomiting, diarrhea, refusal of food, pale gums or tongue, swollen tongue, abdominal pain and convulsions.

Some of the many household substances harmful to your dog.

Help is available from the National Animal Poison Control Center, a division of the American Society for Prevention of Cruelty to Animals. They are available 24 hours a day of every week. Center veterinarians and veterinary toxicologists have up-to-the-minute information on toxicity levels, antidotes, treatments and prognosis based on more than 250,000 cases involving pesticides, drugs, plants, metals and other exposures in pets, livestock and wildlife. These specialists provide advice to animal owners and confer with veterinarians about poison exposures.

If you suspect your Maltese has been poisoned, gather the following information and then call the NAPCC: give your name, address, and telephone number, age, sex, and weight of the animal affected; the substance the animal ingested if known; the time that has elapsed since ingestion and the symptoms the animal is showing.

NAPCC has three telephone numbers for easy access: (900) 680-0000 costs $20 for the first five minutes and $2.95 for each additional minute billed to your telephone; (800) 548-2423 and (888) 426-4435 are credit-card-only numbers for $30 per case. Only MasterCard, Visa, American Express and Discover cards are accepted.

The center also has an animal product safety service for manufacturers of veterinary, agricultural and chemical products. This service provides a toll-free number to be printed on product labels and literature so that toxicity information and treatment advice is available to purchasers. There is no charge for calls made to the number provided on the product. This service also keeps case records, compiles quarterly reports, and works with manufacturers to increase product safety.

Caring for Your Older Maltese

Modern veterinary medicine has made tremendous strides in protecting and repairing the health of family companions, and pets are living longer than ever before. Like people, pets go through life stages of growth, maturity, and aging. The passage from one stage to another is often blurred, and owners must be on guard to recognize the signs that their Maltese is getting old. A Maltese may easily live to be 15 years old or more. A strong, healthy dog will probably age later than a dog that is stressed by disease or environment early in his life. Dogs that are spayed or neutered before 6 months of age ordinarily live longer than dogs that are kept intact.

Good nutrition is critical to good health at all ages. Exercise is also of critical importance in keeping the dog in good shape. Even old dogs generally like to play with a favorite toy for a few minutes each day or take a walk to the corner to get some fresh air. Other steps to delay the onset of aging in dogs include regular teeth cleaning to prevent gum disease; regular grooming to keep his skin and coat healthy and to discover any problems such as dry skin, thin or brittle coat, thin coat, body odor, or sore spots; and checking his ears for odor or buildup produced by infecting organisms.

The first sign of aging is a general decrease in activity level, including a tendency to sleep longer and more soundly, a waning of enthusiasm for long walks and games of catch, and a loss of interest in the goings on in the home.

Older dogs often become less tolerant of extremes in temperature and changes in surroundings. Be sure to keep your aging dog sufficiently warm in the winter and sufficiently cool in the summer. Hearing loss is a frequent consequence of aging, as is some deterioration of sight. Dogs can compensate for these conditions; partial or even total blindness may not be noticed if the dog is in familiar surroundings and has learned to adjust as his eyesight failed.

Older dogs may become less active, but they still like to go out for some fresh air.

Skin and coat change, too, as the skin loses pliability and the capacity of the oil-producing sebaceous glands diminishes. Wounds heal more slowly, allergies often worsen, non-malignant tumors may appear in the mouth or on or under the skin and infestations of intestinal parasite may occur.

As aging advances, heart, liver and kidneys lose their efficiency, and the immune system is less able to fight off attacks by bacteria and viruses. Bladder control may be affected, and muscles decrease in size and function.

Letting Go

There's a fine line to walk between easing your pet's transition into old age and ushering him into the life of a canine invalid. A dog that enjoyed his puppyhood and his mature years should have the opportunity to enjoy his aging years as well.

One of the most difficult decisions to be made in any pet owner's life is the day when he realizes his Maltese has lost his zest for life—his pains and tribulations are too much to bear. Euthanasia is never an easy decision. Sometimes it just makes sense to let go.

Your Happy, Healthy Pet

Your Dog's Name _____

Name on Your Dog's Pedigree (if your dog has one) _____

_____

Where Your Dog Came From _____

_____

Your Dog's Birthday _____

Your Dog's Veterinarian

    Name _____

    Address _____

    Phone Number_____

    Emergency Number_____

Your Dog's Health

    Vaccines

    type _____ date given _____

    type _____ date given _____

    type _____ date given _____

    type _____ date given _____

    Heartworm

    date tested _____ type used_____ start date _____

Your Dog's License Number_____

Groomer's Name and Number _____

Dogsitter/Walker's Name and Number_____

Awards Your Dog Has Won

    Award _____ date earned _____

    Award _____ date earned _____

part three

Enjoying
your
Dog

chapter 8

Basic
Training

by Ian Dunbar, Ph.D., MRCVS

Training is the jewel in the crown—the most important aspect of doggy husbandry. There is no more important variable influencing dog behavior and temperament than the dog's education: A well-trained, well-behaved and good-natured puppydog is always a joy to live with, but an untrained and uncivilized dog can be a perpetual nightmare. Moreover, deny the dog an education and she will not have the opportunity to fulfill her own canine potential; neither will she have the ability to communicate effectively with her human companions.

Luckily, modern psychological training methods are easy, efficient, effective and, above all, considerably dog-friendly and user-friendly.

Doggy education is as simple as it is enjoyable. But before you can have a good time play-training with your new dog, you have to learn what to do and how to do it. There is no bigger variable influencing the success of dog training than the *owner's* experience and expertise. *Before you embark on the dog's education, you must first educate yourself.*

Basic Training for Owners

Ideally, basic owner training should begin well *before* you select your dog. Find out all you can about your chosen breed first, then master rudimentary training and handling skills. If you already have your puppy-dog, owner training is a dire emergency—the clock is ticking! Especially for puppies, the first few weeks at home are the most important and influential days in the dog's life. Indeed, the cause of most adolescent and adult problems may be traced back to the initial days the pup explores her new home. This is the time to establish the *status quo*—to teach the puppydog how you would like her to behave and so prevent otherwise quite predictable problems.

In addition to consulting breeders and breed books such as this one (which understandably have a positive breed bias), seek out as many pet owners with your breed as you can find. Good points are obvious. What you want to find out are the breed-specific *problems*, so you can nip them in the bud. In particular, you should talk to owners with *adolescent* dogs and make a list of all anticipated problems. Most important, *test drive* at least half a dozen adolescent and adult dogs of your breed yourself. An 8-week-old puppy is deceptively easy to handle, but she will acquire adult size, speed and strength in just four months, so you should learn now what to prepare for.

Puppy and pet dog training classes offer a convenient venue to locate pet owners and observe dogs in action. For a list of suitable trainers in your area, contact the Association of Pet Dog Trainers (see chapter 13). You may also begin your basic owner training by observing other owners in class. Watch as many classes and test drive as many dogs as possible. Select an upbeat, dog-friendly, people-friendly, fun-and-games, puppydog pet training class to learn the ropes. Also, watch training videos and read training books. You must find out what to do and how to do it *before* you have to do it.

Principles of Training

Most people think training comprises teaching the dog to do things such as sit, speak and roll over, but even a 4-week-old pup knows how to do these things already. Instead, the first step in training involves teaching the dog human words for each dog behavior and activity and for each aspect of the dog's environment. That way you, the owner, can more easily participate in the dog's domestic education by directing her to perform specific actions appropriately, that is, at the right time, in the right place and so on. Training opens communication channels, enabling an educated dog to at least understand her owner's requests.

In addition to teaching a dog *what* we want her to do, it is also necessary to teach her *why* she should do what we ask. Indeed, 95 percent of training revolves around motivating the dog *to want to do* what we want. Dogs often understand what their owners want; they just don't see the point of doing it—especially when the owner's repetitively boring and seemingly senseless instructions are totally at odds with much more pressing and exciting doggy distractions. It is not so much the dog that is being stubborn or dominant; rather, it is the owner who has failed to acknowledge the dog's needs and feelings and to approach training from the dog's point of view.

THE MEANING OF INSTRUCTIONS

The secret to successful training is learning how to use training lures to predict or prompt specific behaviors—to coax the dog to do what you want *when* you want. Any highly valued object (such as a treat or toy) may be used as a lure, which the dog will follow with her eyes and nose. Moving the lure in specific ways entices the dog to move her nose, head and entire body in specific ways. In fact, by learning the art of manipulating various lures, it is possible to teach the dog to assume virtually any body position and perform any action. Once you have control over the expression of the dog's behaviors and can elicit any body position or behavior at will, you can easily teach the dog to perform on request.

Teach your dog words for each activity she needs to know, like down.

Tell your dog what you want her to do, use a lure to entice her to respond correctly, then profusely praise and maybe reward her once she performs the desired action. For example, verbally request "Tina, sit!" while you move a squeaky toy upwards and backwards over the dog's muzzle (lure-movement and hand signal), smile knowingly as she looks up (to follow the lure) and sits down (as a result of canine anatomical engineering), then praise her to distraction ("Gooood Tina!"). Squeak the toy, offer a training treat and give your dog and yourself a pat on the back.

Being able to elicit desired responses over and over enables the owner to reward the dog over and over. Consequently, the dog begins to think training is fun. For example, the more the dog is rewarded for sitting, the more she enjoys sitting. Eventually the dog comes to realize that, whereas most sitting is appreciated, sitting immediately upon request usually prompts especially enthusiastic praise and a slew of high-level rewards. The dog begins to sit on cue much of the time, showing that she is starting to grasp the meaning of the owner's verbal request and hand signal.

WHY COMPLY?

Most dogs enjoy initial lure-reward training and are only too happy to comply with their owners' wishes. Unfortunately, repetitive drilling without appreciative feedback tends to diminish the dog's enthusiasm until she eventually fails to see the point of complying anymore. Moreover, as the dog approaches adolescence she becomes more easily distracted as she develops other interests. Lengthy sessions with repetitive exercises tend to bore and demotivate both parties. If it's not fun, the owner doesn't do it and neither does the dog.

Integrate training into your dog's life: The greater number of training sessions each day and the *shorter* they are, the more willingly compliant your dog will

become. Make sure to have a short (just a few seconds) training interlude before every enjoyable canine activity. For example, ask your dog to sit to greet people, to sit before you throw her Frisbee and to sit for her supper. Really, sitting is no different from a canine "Please."

To train your dog, you need gentle hands, a loving heart and a good attitude.

Also, include numerous short training interludes during every enjoyable canine pastime, for example, when playing with the dog or when she is running in the park. In this fashion, doggy distractions may be effectively converted into rewards for training. Just as all games have rules, fun becomes training . . . and training becomes fun.

Eventually, rewards actually become unnecessary to continue motivating your dog. If trained with consideration and kindness, performing the desired behaviors will become self-rewarding and, in a sense, your dog will motivate herself. Just as it is not necessary to reward a human companion during an enjoyable walk in the park, or following a game of tennis, it is hardly necessary to reward our best friend—the dog— for walking by our side or while playing fetch. Human company during enjoyable activities is reward enough for most dogs.

Even though your dog has become self-motivating, it's still good to praise and pet her a lot and offer rewards once in a while, especially for a good job well done. And if for no other reason, praising and rewarding others is good for the human heart.

PUNISHMENT

Without a doubt, lure-reward training is by far the best way to teach: Entice your dog to do what you want and then reward her for doing so. Unfortunately, a human shortcoming is to take the good for granted and to moan and groan at the bad. Specifically, the dog's many good behaviors are ignored while the owner focuses on punishing the dog for making mistakes. In extreme cases, instruction is *limited* to punishing mistakes made by a trainee dog, child, employee or husband, even though it has been proven punishment training is notoriously inefficient and ineffective and is decidedly unfriendly and combative. It teaches the dog that training is a drag, almost as quickly as it teaches the dog to dislike her trainer. Why treat our best friends like our worst enemies?

Punishment training is also much more laborious and time consuming. Whereas it takes only a finite amount of time to teach a dog what to chew, for example, it takes much, much longer to punish the dog for each and every mistake. Remember, *there is only one right way!* So why not teach that right way from the outset?!

To make matters worse, punishment training causes severe lapses in the dog's reliability. Since it is obviously impossible to punish the dog each and every time she misbehaves, the dog quickly learns to distinguish between those times when she must comply (so as to avoid impending punishment) and those times when she need not comply, because punishment is impossible. Such times include when the dog is off leash and 6 feet away, when the owner is otherwise engaged (talking to a friend, watching television, taking a shower, tending to the baby or chatting on the telephone) or when the dog is left at home alone.

Instances of misbehavior will be numerous when the owner is away, because even when the dog complied in the owner's looming presence, she did so unwillingly. The dog was forced to act against her will, rather than molding her will to want to please. Hence, when the owner is absent, not only does the dog know she need not comply, she simply does not want to. Again, the trainee is not a stubborn vindictive beast, but rather the trainer has failed to teach. Punishment training invariably creates unpredictable Jekyll and Hyde behavior.

Trainer's Tools

Many training books extol the virtues of a vast array of training paraphernalia and electronic and metallic gizmos, most of which are designed for canine restraint, correction and punishment, rather than for actual facilitation of doggy education. In reality, most effective training tools are not found in stores; they come from within ourselves. In addition to a willing dog, all you really need is a functional human brain, gentle hands, a loving heart and a good attitude.

In terms of equipment, all dogs do require a quality buckle collar to sport dog tags and to attach the leash (for safety and to comply with local leash laws). Hollow chew toys (like Kongs or sterilized longbones) and a dog bed or collapsible crate are musts for housetraining. Three additional tools are required:

1. specific lures (training treats and toys) to predict and prompt specific desired behaviors;

2. rewards (praise, affection, training treats and toys) to reinforce for the dog what a lot of fun it all is; and

3. knowledge—how to convert the dog's favorite activities and games (potential distractions to training) into "life-rewards," which may be employed to facilitate training.

The most powerful of these is *knowledge*. Education is the key! Watch training classes, participate in training classes, watch videos, read books, enjoy play-training with your dog and then your dog will say "Please," and your dog will say "Thank you!"

Housetraining

If dogs were left to their own devices, certainly they would chew, dig and bark for entertainment and then no doubt highlight a few areas of their living space with sprinkles of urine, in much the same way we decorate by hanging pictures. Consequently, when we ask a dog to live with us, we must teach her *where* she may dig, *where* she may perform her toilet duties, *what* she may chew and *when* she may bark. After all, when left at home alone for many hours, we cannot expect the dog to amuse herself by completing crosswords or watching the soaps on TV!

Also, it would be decidedly unfair to keep the house rules a secret from the dog, and then get angry and punish the poor critter for inevitably transgressing rules she did not even know existed. Remember: Without adequate education and guidance, the dog will be forced to establish her own rules—doggy rules—and most probably will be at odds with the owner's view of domestic living.

Since most problems develop during the first few days the dog is at home, prospective dog owners must be certain they are quite clear about the principles of housetraining *before* they get a dog. Early misbehaviors quickly become established as the *status quo*—

becoming firmly entrenched as hard-to-break bad habits, which set the precedent for years to come. Make sure to teach your dog good habits right from the start. Good habits are just as hard to break as bad ones!

Ideally, when a new dog comes home, try to arrange for someone to be present as much as possible during the first few days (for adult dogs) or weeks for puppies. With only a little forethought, it is surprisingly easy to find a puppy sitter, such as a retired person, who would be willing to eat from your refrigerator and watch your television while keeping an eye on the newcomer to encourage the dog to play with chew toys and to ensure she goes outside on a regular basis.

POTTY TRAINING

To teach the dog where to relieve herself:

1. never let her make a single mistake;
2. let her know where you want her to go; and
3. handsomely reward her for doing so: "GOOOOOOOD DOG!!!" liver treat, liver treat, liver treat!

Preventing Mistakes

A single mistake is a training disaster, since it heralds many more in future weeks. And each time the dog soils the house, this further reinforces the dog's unfortunate preference for an indoor, carpeted toilet. *Do not let an unhousetrained dog have full run of the house.*

When you are away from home, or cannot pay full attention, confine the dog to an area where elimination is appropriate, such as an outdoor run or, better still, a small, comfortable indoor kennel with access to an outdoor run. When confined in this manner, most dogs will naturally housetrain themselves.

If that's not possible, confine the dog to an area, such as a utility room, kitchen, basement or garage, where elimination may not be desired in the long run but as an interim measure it is certainly preferable to doing it all around the house. Use newspaper to cover the floor of the dog's day room. The newspaper may be used to soak up the urine and to wrap up and dispose of the feces. Once your dog develops a preferred spot for eliminating, it is only necessary to cover that part of the floor with newspaper. The smaller papered area may then be moved (only a little each day) towards the door to the outside. Thus the dog will develop the tendency to go to the door when she needs to relieve herself.

Never confine an unhousetrained dog to a crate for long periods. Doing so would force the dog to soil the crate and ruin its usefulness as an aid for housetraining (see the following discussion).

Teaching Where

In order to teach your dog where you would like her to do her business, you have to be there to direct the proceedings—an obvious, yet often neglected, fact of life. In order to be there to teach the dog *where* to go, you need to know *when* she needs to go. Indeed, the success of housetraining depends on the owner's ability to predict these times. Certainly, a regular feeding schedule will facilitate prediction somewhat, but there is nothing like "loading the deck" and influencing the timing of the outcome yourself!

Whenever you are at home, make sure the dog is under constant supervision and/or confined to a small

The first few weeks at home are the most important and influential in your dog's life.

area. If already well trained, simply instruct the dog to lie down in her bed or basket. Alternatively, confine the dog to a crate (doggy den) or tie-down (a short, 18-inch lead that can be clipped to an eye hook in the baseboard near her bed). Short-term close confinement strongly inhibits urination and defecation, since the dog does not want to soil her sleeping area. Thus, when you release the puppydog each hour, she will definitely need to urinate immediately and defecate every third or fourth hour. Keep the dog confined to her doggy den and take her to her intended toilet area each hour, every hour and on the hour.

When taking your dog outside, instruct her to sit quietly before opening the door—she will soon learn to sit by the door when she needs to go out!

Teaching Why

Being able to predict when the dog needs to go enables the owner to be on the spot to praise and reward the dog. Each hour, hurry the dog to the intended toilet area in the yard, issue the appropriate instruction ("Go pee!" or "Go poop!"), then give the dog three to four minutes to produce. Praise and offer a couple of training treats when successful. The treats are important because many people fail to praise their dogs with feeling . . . and housetraining is hardly the time for understatement. So either loosen up and enthusiastically praise that dog: "Wuzzzer-wuzzer-wuzzer, hoooser good wuffer den? Hoooo went pee for Daddy?" Or say "Good dog!" as best you can and offer the treats for effect.

Following elimination is an ideal time for a spot of play-training in the yard or house. Also, an empty dog may be allowed greater freedom around the house for the next half hour or so, just as long as you keep an eye out to make sure she does not get into other kinds of mischief. If you are preoccupied and cannot pay full attention, confine the dog to her doggy den once more to enjoy a peaceful snooze or to play with her many chew toys.

If your dog does not eliminate within the allotted time outside—no biggie! Back to her doggy den, and then try again after another hour.

As I own large dogs, I always feel more relaxed walking an empty dog, knowing that I will not need to finish our stroll weighted down with bags of feces!

Beware of falling into the trap of walking the dog to get her to eliminate. The good ol' dog walk is such an enormous highlight in the dog's life that it represents the single biggest potential reward in domestic dogdom. However, when in a hurry, or during inclement weather, many owners abruptly terminate the walk the moment the dog has done her business. This, in effect, severely punishes the dog for doing the right thing, in the right place at the right time. Consequently, many dogs become strongly inhibited from eliminating outdoors because they know it will signal an abrupt end to an otherwise thoroughly enjoyable walk.

Instead, instruct the dog to relieve herself in the yard prior to going for a walk. If you follow the above instructions, most dogs soon learn to eliminate on cue. As soon as the dog eliminates, praise (and offer a treat or two)—"Good dog! Let's go walkies!" Use the walk as a reward for eliminating in the yard. If the dog does not go, put her back in her doggy den and think about a walk later on. You will find with a "No feces—no walk" policy, your dog will become one of the fastest defecators in the business.

If you do not have a backyard, instruct the dog to eliminate right outside your front door prior to the walk. Not only will this facilitate clean up and disposal of the feces in your own trash can but, also, the walk may again be used as a colossal reward.

CHEWING AND BARKING

Short-term close confinement also teaches the dog that occasional quiet moments are a reality of domestic living. Your puppydog is extremely impressionable during her first few weeks at home. Regular confinement at this time soon exerts a calming influence over the dog's personality. Remember, once the dog is housetrained and calmer, there will be a whole lifetime ahead for the dog to enjoy full run of the house and garden. On the other hand, by letting the newcomer have unrestricted access to the entire household and allowing her to run willy-nilly, she will most certainly develop a bunch of behavior problems in short order, no doubt necessitating confinement later in life. It would not be fair to remedially restrain and confine a dog you have trained, through neglect, to run free.

When confining the dog, make sure she always has an impressive array of suitable chew toys. Kongs and sterilized longbones (both readily available from pet stores) make the best chew toys, since they are hollow and may be stuffed with treats to heighten the dog's interest. For example, by stuffing the little hole at the top of a Kong with a small piece of freeze-dried liver, the dog will not want to leave it alone.

Remember, treats do not have to be junk food and they certainly should not represent extra calories. Rather, treats should be part of each dog's regular daily diet: Some food may be served in the dog's bowl for breakfast and dinner, some food may be used as training treats, and some food may be used for stuffing chew toys. I regularly stuff my dogs' many Kongs with different shaped biscuits and kibble.

Make sure your puppy has suitable chew toys.

The kibble seems to fall out fairly easily, as do the oval-shaped biscuits, thus rewarding the dog instantaneously for checking out the chew toys. The bone-shaped biscuits fall out after a while, rewarding the dog for worrying at the chew toy. But the triangular biscuits never come out. They remain inside the Kong as lures, maintaining the dog's fascination with her chew toy. To further focus the dog's interest, I always make sure to flavor the triangular biscuits by rubbing them with a little cheese or freeze-dried liver.

To teach come, call your dog, open your arms as a welcoming signal, wave a toy or a treat and praise for every step in your direction.

If stuffed chew toys are reserved especially for times the dog is confined, the puppydog will soon learn to enjoy quiet moments in her doggy den and she will quickly develop a chew-toy habit— a good habit! This is a simple *autoshaping* process; all the owner has to do is set up the situation and the dog all but trains herself— easy and effective. Even when the dog is given run of the house, her first inclination will be to indulge her rewarding chew-toy habit rather than destroy less-attractive household articles, such as curtains, carpets, chairs and compact disks. Similarly, a chew-toy chewer will be less inclined to scratch and chew herself excessively. Also, if the dog busies herself as a recreational chewer, she will be less inclined to develop into a recreational barker or digger when left at home alone.

Stuff a number of chew toys whenever the dog is left confined and remove the extra-special-tasting treats when you return. Your dog will now amuse herself with her chew toys before falling asleep and then resume playing with her chew toys when she expects you to return. Since most owner-absent misbehavior happens right after you leave and right before your expected return, your puppydog will now be conveniently preoccupied with her chew toys at these times.

Come and Sit

Most puppies will happily approach virtually anyone, whether called or not; that is, until they collide with adolescence and

develop other more important doggy interests, such as sniffing a multiplicity of exquisite odors on the grass. Your mission, Mr./Ms. Owner, is to teach and reward the pup for coming reliably, willingly and happily when called—and you have just three months to get it done. Unless adequately reinforced, your puppy's tendency to approach people will self-destruct by adolescence.

Call your dog ("Tina, come!"), open your arms (and maybe squat down) as a welcoming signal, waggle a treat or toy as a lure and reward the puppydog when she comes running. Do not wait to praise the dog until she reaches you—she may come 95 percent of the way and then run off after some distraction. Instead, praise the dog's *first* step towards you and continue praising enthusiastically for *every* step she takes in your direction.

When the rapidly approaching puppy dog is three lengths away from impact, instruct her to sit ("Tina, sit!") and hold the lure in front of you in an outstretched hand to prevent her from hitting you midchest and knocking you flat on your back! As Tina decelerates to nose the lure, move the treat upwards and backwards just over her muzzle with an upwards motion of your extended arm (palm-upwards). As the dog looks up to follow the lure, she will sit down (if she jumps up, you are holding the lure too high). Praise the dog for sitting. Move backwards and call her again. Repeat this many times over, always praising when Tina comes and sits; on occasion, reward her.

For the first couple of trials, use a training treat both as a lure to entice the dog to come and sit and as a reward for doing so. Thereafter, try to use different items as lures and rewards. For example, lure the dog with a Kong or Frisbee but reward her with a food treat. Or lure the dog with a food treat but pat her and throw a tennis ball as a reward. After just a few repetitions, dispense with the lures and rewards; the dog will begin to respond willingly to your verbal requests and hand signals just for the prospect of praise from your heart and affection from your hands.

Instruct every family member, friend and visitor how to get the dog to come and sit. Invite people over for a series of pooch parties; do not keep the pup a secret— let other people enjoy this puppy, and let the pup enjoy other people. Puppydog parties are not only fun, they easily attract a lot of people to help *you* train *your* dog. Unless you teach your dog how to meet people, that is, to sit for greetings, no doubt the dog will resort to jumping up. Then you and the visitors will get annoyed, and the dog will be punished. This is not fair. *Send out those invitations for puppy parties and teach your dog to be mannerly and socially acceptable.*

Even though your dog quickly masters obedient recalls in the house, her reliability may falter when playing in the backyard or local park. Ironically, it is *the owner* who has unintentionally trained the dog *not* to respond in these instances. By allowing the dog to play and run around and otherwise have a good time, but then to call the dog to put her on leash to take her home, the dog quickly learns playing is fun but training is a drag. Thus, playing in the park becomes a severe distraction, which works against training. Bad news!

Instead, whether playing with the dog off leash or on leash, request her to come at frequent intervals—say, every minute or so. On most occasions, praise and pet the dog for a few seconds while she is sitting, then tell her to go play again. For especially fast recalls, offer a couple of training treats and take the time to praise and pet the dog enthusiastically before releasing her. The dog will learn that coming when called is not necessarily the end of the play session, and neither is it the end of the world; rather, it signals an enjoyable, quality time-out with the owner before resuming play once more. In fact, playing in the park now becomes a very effective life-reward, which works to facilitate training by reinforcing each obedient and timely recall. Good news!

Sit, Down, Stand and Rollover

Teaching the dog a variety of body positions is easy for owner and dog, impressive for spectators and extremely useful for all. Using lure-reward techniques, it is possible to train several positions at once to verbal commands or hand signals (which impress the socks off onlookers).

Sit and ***down***—the two control commands—prevent or resolve nearly a hundred behavior problems. For example, if the dog happily and obediently sits or lies down when requested, she cannot jump on visitors, dash out the front door, run around and chase her tail, pester other dogs, harass cats or annoy family, friends or strangers. Additionally, "Sit" or "Down" are the best emergency commands for off-leash control.

It is easier to teach and maintain a reliable sit than maintain a reliable recall. *Sit* is the purest and simplest of commands—either the dog is sitting or she is not. If there is any change of circumstances or potential danger in the park, for example, simply instruct the dog to sit. If she sits, you have a number of options: Allow the dog to resume playing when she is safe, walk up and put the dog on leash or call the dog. The dog will be much more likely to come when called if she has already acknowledged her compliance by sitting. If the dog does not sit in the park—train her to!

Stand and ***rollover-stay*** are the two positions for examining the dog. Your veterinarian will love you to distraction if you take a little time to teach the dog to stand still and roll over and play possum. Also, your vet bills will be smaller because it will take the veterinarian less time to examine your dog. The rollover-stay is an especially useful command and is really just a variation of the down-stay: Whereas the dog lies prone in the traditional down, she lies supine in the rollover-stay.

As with teaching come and sit, the training techniques to teach the dog to assume all other body positions on cue are user-friendly and dog-friendly. Simply give the appropriate request, lure the dog into the desired body position using a training treat or toy and then *praise* (and maybe reward) the dog as soon as she complies. Try not to touch the dog to get her to respond. If you teach the dog by guiding her into position, the dog will quickly learn that rump-pressure means sit, for example, but as yet you still have no control over your dog if she is just 6 feet away. It will still be necessary to teach the dog to sit on request. So do not make training a time-consuming two-step process; instead, teach the dog to sit to a verbal request or hand signal from the outset. Once the dog sits willingly when requested, by all means use your hands to pet the dog when she does so.

To teach *down* when the dog is already sitting, say "Tina, down!," hold the lure in one hand (palm down) and lower that hand to the floor between the dog's forepaws. As the dog lowers her head to follow the lure, slowly move the lure away from the dog just a fraction (in front of her paws). The dog will lie down as she stretches her nose forward to follow the lure. Praise the dog when she does so. If the dog stands up, you pulled the lure away too far and too quickly.

When teaching the dog to lie down from the standing position, say "Down" and lower the lure to the floor as before. Once the dog has lowered her forequarters and assumed a play bow, gently and slowly move the lure *towards* the dog between her forelegs. Praise the dog as soon as her rear end plops down.

After just a couple of trials it will be possible to alternate sits and downs and have the dog energetically perform doggy push-ups. Praise the dog a lot, and after half a dozen or so push-ups reward the dog with a training treat or toy. You will notice the more energetically you move your arm—upwards (palm up) to get the dog to sit, and downwards (palm down) to get the dog to lie down—the more energetically the dog responds to your requests. Now try training the dog in silence and you will notice she has also learned to respond to hand signals. Yeah! Not too shabby for the first session.

To teach *stand* from the sitting position, say "Tina, stand," slowly move the lure half a dog-length away from the dog's nose, keeping it at nose level, and praise the dog as she stands to follow the lure. As soon

Using a food lure to teach sit, down and stand. 1) "Phoenix, sit." 2) Hand palm upwards, move lure up and back over dog's muzzle. 3) "Good sit, Phoenix!" 4) "Phoenix, down." 5) Hand palm downwards, move lure down to lie between dog's forepaws. 6) "Phoenix, off. Good down, Phoenix!" 7) "Phoenix, sit!" 8) Palm upwards, move lure up and back, keeping it close to dog's muzzle. 9) "Good sit, Phoenix!"

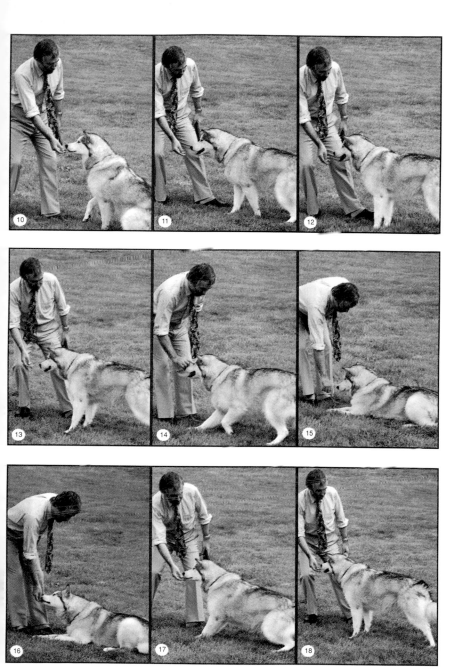

10) *"Phoenix, stand!"* 11) *Move lure away from dog at nose height, then lower it a tad.* 12) *"Phoenix, off! Good stand, Phoenix!"* 13) *"Phoenix, down!"* 14) *Hand palm downwards, move lure down to lie between dog's forepaws.* 15) *"Phoenix, off! Good down-stay, Phoenix!"* 16) *"Phoenix, stand!"* 17) *Move lure away from dog's muzzle up to nose height.* 18) *"Phoenix, off! Good stand-stay, Phoenix. Now we'll make the vet and groomer happy!"*

as the dog stands, lower the lure to just beneath the dog's chin to entice her to look down; otherwise she will stand and then sit immediately. To prompt the dog to stand from the down position, move the lure half a dog-length upwards and away from the dog, holding the lure at standing nose height from the floor.

Teaching *rollover* is best started from the down position, with the dog lying on one side, or at least with both hind legs stretched out on the same side. Say "Tina, bang!" and move the lure backwards and alongside the dog's muzzle to her elbow (on the side of her outstretched hind legs). Once the dog looks to the side and backwards, very slowly move the lure upwards to the dog's shoulder and backbone. Tickling the dog in the goolies (groin area) often invokes a reflex-raising of the hind leg as an appeasement gesture, which facilitates the tendency to roll over. If you move the lure too quickly and the dog jumps into the standing position, have patience and start again. As soon as the dog rolls onto her back, keep the lure stationary and mesmerize the dog with a relaxing tummy rub.

To teach *rollover-stay* when the dog is standing or moving, say "Tina, bang!" and give the appropriate hand signal (with index finger pointed and thumb cocked in true Sam Spade fashion), then in one fluid movement lure her to first lie down and then rollover-stay as above.

Teaching the dog to *stay* in each of the above four positions becomes a piece of cake after first teaching the dog not to worry at the toy or treat training lure. This is best accomplished by hand feeding dinner kibble. Hold a piece of kibble firmly in your hand and softly instruct "Off!" Ignore any licking and slobbering *for however long the dog worries at the treat*, but say "Take it!" and offer the kibble *the instant* the dog breaks contact with her muzzle. Repeat this a few times, and then up the ante and insist the dog remove her muzzle for one whole second before offering the kibble. Then progressively refine your criteria and have the dog not touch your hand (or treat) for longer and longer periods on each trial, such as for two seconds, four seconds, then six, ten, fifteen, twenty, thirty seconds and so on.

The dog soon learns: (1) worrying at the treat never gets results, whereas (2) noncontact is often rewarded after a variable time lapse.

Teaching *"Off!"* has many useful applications in its own right. Additionally, instructing the dog not to touch a training lure often produces spontaneous and magical stays. Request the dog to stand-stay, for example, and not to touch the lure. At first set your sights on a short two-second stay before rewarding the dog. (Remember, every long journey begins with a single step.) However, on subsequent trials, gradually and progressively increase the length of stay required to receive a reward. In no time at all your dog will stand calmly for a minute or so.

Relevancy Training

Once you have taught the dog what you expect her to do when requested to come, sit, lie down, stand, rollover and stay, the time is right to teach the dog *why* she should comply with your wishes. The secret is to have many (*many*) extremely short training interludes (two to five seconds each) at numerous (*numerous*) times during the course of the dog's day. Especially work with the dog immediately *before* the dog's good times and *during* the dog's good times. For example, ask your dog to sit and/or lie down each time before opening doors, serving meals, offering treats and tummy rubs; ask the dog to perform a few controlled doggy push-ups before letting her off leash or throwing a tennis ball; and perhaps request the dog to sit-down-sit-stand-down-stand-rollover before inviting her to cuddle on the couch.

Similarly, request the dog to sit many times during play or on walks, and in no time at all the dog will be only too pleased to follow your instructions because she has learned that a compliant response heralds all sorts of goodies. Basically all you are trying to teach the dog is how to say please: "Please throw the tennis ball. Please may I snuggle on the couch."

Remember, it is important to keep training interludes short and to have many short sessions each and every day. The shortest (and most useful) session comprises asking the dog to sit and then go play during a play session. When trained this way, your dog will soon associate training with good times. In fact, the dog may be unable to distinguish between training and good times and, indeed, there should be no distinction. The warped concept that training involves forcing the dog to comply and/or dominating her will is totally at odds with the picture of a truly well-trained dog. In reality, enjoying a game of training with a dog is no different from enjoying a game of backgammon or tennis with a friend; and walking with a dog should be no different from strolling with a spouse, or with buddies on the golf course.

Walk by Your Side

Many people attempt to teach a dog to heel by putting her on a leash and physically correcting the dog when she makes mistakes. There are a number of things seriously wrong with this approach, the first being that most people do not want precision heeling; rather, they simply want the dog to follow or walk by their side. Second, when physically restrained during "training," even though the dog may grudgingly mope by your side when "handcuffed" on leash, let's see what happens when she is off leash. History! The dog is in the next county because she never enjoyed walking with you on leash and you have no control over her off leash. So let's just teach the dog off leash from the outset to *want* to walk with us. Third, if the dog has not been trained to heel, it is a trifle hasty to think about punishing the poor dog for making mistakes and breaking heeling rules she didn't even know existed. This is simply not fair! Surely, if the dog had been adequately taught how to heel, she would seldom make mistakes and hence there would be no need to correct the dog. Remember, each mistake and each correction (punishment) advertise the trainer's inadequacy, not the dog's. The dog is not stubborn, she is not stupid and she is not bad. Even if she were, she would still require training, so let's train her properly.

Let's teach the dog to *enjoy* following us and to *want* to walk by our side off leash. Then it will be easier to teach high-precision off-leash heeling patterns if desired. Before going on outdoor walks, it is necessary to teach the dog not to pull. Then it becomes easy to teach on-leash walking and heeling because the dog already wants to walk with you, she is familiar with the desired walking and heeling positions and she knows not to pull.

FOLLOWING

Start by training your dog to follow you. Many puppies will follow if you simply walk away from them and maybe click your fingers or chuckle. Adult dogs may require additional enticement to stimulate them to follow, such as a training lure or, at the very least, a lively trainer. To teach the dog to follow: (1) keep walking and (2) walk away from the dog. If the dog attempts to lead or lag, change pace; slow down if the dog forges too far ahead, but speed up if she lags too far behind. Say "Steady!" or "Easy!" each time before you slow down and "Quickly!" or "Hustle!" each time before you speed up, and the dog will learn to change pace on cue. If the dog lags or leads too far, or if she wanders right or left, simply walk quickly in the opposite direction and maybe even run away from the dog and hide.

Practicing is a lot of fun; you can set up a course in your home, yard or park to do this. Indoors, entice the dog to follow upstairs, into a bedroom, into the bathroom, downstairs, around the living room couch, zigzagging between dining room chairs and into the kitchen for dinner. Outdoors, get the dog to follow around park benches, trees, shrubs and along walkways and lines in the grass. (For safety outdoors, it is advisable to attach a long line on the dog, but never exert corrective tension on the line.)

Remember, following has a lot to do with attitude—
your attitude! Most probably your dog will *not* want to
follow Mr. Grumpy Troll with the personality of wilted
lettuce. Lighten up—walk with a jaunty step, whistle a
happy tune, sing, skip and tell jokes to your dog and
she will be right there by your side.

By Your Side

It is smart to train the dog to walk close on one side or
the other—either side will do, your choice. When walking, jogging or cycling, it is generally bad news to have
the dog suddenly cut in front of you. In fact, I train my
dogs to walk "By my side" and "Other side"—both very
useful instructions. It is possible to position the dog
fairly accurately by looking to the appropriate side and
clicking your fingers or slapping your thigh on that
side. A precise positioning may be attained by holding
a training lure, such as a chew toy, tennis ball or food
treat. Stop and stand still several times throughout the
walk, just as you would when window shopping or
meeting a friend. Use the lure to make sure the dog
slows down and stays close whenever you stop.

When teaching the dog to heel, we generally want
her to sit in heel position when we stop. Teach heel

*Using a toy to teach sit-heel-sit sequences: 1) "Phoenix, sit!" Standing still, move lure up and back over dog's
muzzle . . . 2) to position dog sitting in heel position on your left side. 3) Say "Phoenix,heel!" and walk ahead,
wagging lure in left hand. Change lure to right hand in preparation for sit signal. Say "Sit" and then . . .*

position at the standstill and the dog will learn that the default heel position is sitting by your side (left or right—your choice, unless you wish to compete in obedience trials, in which case the dog must heel on the left).

Several times a day, stand up and call your dog to come and sit in heel position—"Tina, heel!" For example, instruct the dog to come to heel each time there are commercials on TV, or each time you turn a page of a novel, and the dog will get it in a single evening.

Practice straight-line heeling and turns separately. With the dog sitting at heel, teach her to turn in place. After each quarter-turn, half-turn or full turn in place, lure the dog to sit at heel. Now it's time for short straight-line heeling sequences, no more than a few steps at a time. Always think of heeling in terms of sit-heel-sit sequences—start and end with the dog in position and do your best to keep her there when moving. Progressively increase the number of steps in each sequence. When the dog remains close for 20 yards of straight-line heeling, it is time to add a few turns and then sign up for a happy-heeling obedience class to get some advice from the experts.

4) use hand signal to lure dog to sit as you stop. Eventually, dog will sit automatically at heel whenever you stop. 5) "Good dog!"

No Pulling on Leash

You can start teaching your dog not to pull on leash anywhere—in front of the television or outdoors—but regardless of location, you must not take a single step with tension in the leash. For a reason known only to dogs, even just a couple of paces of pulling on leash is intrinsically motivating and diabolically rewarding. Instead, attach the leash to the dog's collar, grasp the other end firmly with both hands held close to your chest, and stand still—do not budge an inch. Have somebody watch you with a stopwatch to time your progress, or else you will never believe this will work and so you will not even try the exercise, and your shoulder and the dog's neck will be traumatized for years to come.

Stand still and wait for the dog to stop pulling, and to sit and/or lie down. All dogs stop pulling and sit eventually. Most take only a couple of minutes; the all-time record is 22½ minutes. Time how long it takes. Gently praise the dog when she stops pulling, and as soon as she sits, enthusiastically praise the dog and take just one step forward, then immediately stand still. This single step usually demonstrates the ballistic reinforcing nature of pulling on leash; most dogs explode to the end of the leash, so be prepared for the strain. Stand firm and wait for the dog to sit again. Repeat this half a dozen times and you will probably notice a progressive reduction in the force of the dog's one-step explosions and a radical reduction in the time it takes for the dog to sit each time.

As the dog learns "Sit we go" and "Pull we stop," she will begin to walk forward calmly with each single step and automatically sit when you stop. Now try two steps before you stop. Wooooooo! Scary! When the dog has mastered two steps at a time, try for three. After each success, progressively increase the number of steps in the sequence: try four steps and then six, eight, ten and twenty steps before stopping. Congratulations! You are now walking the dog on leash.

Whenever walking with the dog (off leash or on leash), make sure you stop periodically to practice a few position commands and stays before instructing the dog to "Walk on!" (Remember, you want the dog to be compliant everywhere, not just in the kitchen when her dinner is at hand.) For example, stopping every 25 yards to briefly train the dog amounts to over 200 training interludes within a single 3-mile stroll. And each training session is in a different location. You will not believe the improvement within just the first mile of the first walk.

To put it another way, integrating training into a walk offers 200 separate opportunities to use the continuance of the walk as a reward to reinforce the dog's education. Moreover, some training interludes may comprise continuing education for the dog's walking skills: Alternate short periods of the dog walking calmly by your side with periods when the dog is allowed to sniff and investigate the environment. Now sniffing odors on the grass and meeting other dogs become rewards which reinforce the dog's calm and mannerly demeanor. Good Lord! Whatever next? Many enjoyable walks together of course. Happy trails!

THE IMPORTANCE OF TRICKS

Nothing will improve a dog's quality of life better than having a few tricks under her belt. Teaching any trick expands the dog's vocabulary, which facilitates communication and improves the owner's control. Also, specific tricks help prevent and resolve specific behavior problems. For example, by teaching the dog to fetch her toys, the dog learns carrying a toy makes the owner happy and, therefore, will be more likely to chew her toy than other inappropriate items.

More important, teaching tricks prompts owners to lighten up and train with a sunny disposition. Really, tricks should be no different from any other behaviors we put on cue. But they are. When teaching tricks, owners have a much sweeter attitude, which in turn motivates the dog and improves her willingness to comply. The dog feels tricks are a blast, but formal commands are a drag. In fact, tricks are so enjoyable, they may be used as rewards in training by asking the dog to come, sit and down-stay and then rollover for a tummy rub. Go on, try it: Crack a smile and even giggle when the dog promptly and willingly lies down and stays.

Most important, performing tricks prompts onlookers to smile and giggle. Many people are scared of dogs, especially large ones. And nothing can be more off-putting for a dog than to be constantly confronted by strangers who don't like her because of her size or the way she looks. Uneasy people put the dog on edge, causing her to back off and bark, only frightening people all the more. And so a vicious circle develops, with the people's fear fueling the dog's fear *and vice versa*. Instead, tie a pink ribbon to your dog's collar and practice all sorts of tricks on walks and in the park, and you will be pleasantly amazed how it changes people's attitudes toward your friendly dog. The dog's repertoire of tricks is limited only by the trainer's imagination. Below I have described three of my favorites:

SPEAK AND SHUSH

The training sequence involved in teaching a dog to bark on request is no different from that used when training any behavior on cue: request—lure—response—reward. As always, the secret of success lies in finding an effective lure. If the dog always barks at the doorbell, for example, say "Rover, speak!", have an accomplice ring the doorbell, then reward the dog for barking. After a few woofs, ask Rover to "Shush!", waggle a food treat under her nose (to entice her to sniff and thus to shush), praise her when quiet and eventually offer the treat as a reward. Alternate "Speak" and "Shush," progressively increasing the length of shush-time between each barking bout.

PLAY BOW

With the dog standing, say "Bow!" and lower the food lure (palm upwards) to rest between the dog's forepaws. Praise as the dog lowers

her forequarters and sternum to the ground (as when teaching the down), but then lure the dog to stand and offer the treat. On successive trials, gradually increase the length of time the dog is required to remain in the play bow posture in order to gain a food reward. If the dog's rear end collapses into a down, say nothing and offer no reward; simply start over.

BE A BEAR

With the dog sitting backed into a corner to prevent her from toppling over backwards, say "Be a bear!" With bent paw and palm down, raise a lure upwards and backwards along the top of the dog's muzzle. Praise the dog when she sits up on her haunches and offer the treat as a reward. To prevent the dog from standing on her hind legs, keep the lure closer to the dog's muzzle. On each trial, progressively increase the length of time the dog is required to sit up to receive a food reward. Since lure-reward training is so easy, teach the dog to stand and walk on her hind legs as well!

Teaching "Be a Bear"

chapter 9

Getting
Active
with your Dog

by Bardi McLennan

Once you and your dog have graduated from basic obedience training and are beginning to work together as a team, you can take part in the growing world of dog activities. There are so many fun things to do with your dog! Just remember, people and dogs don't always learn at the same pace, so don't be upset if you (or your dog) need more than two basic training courses before your team becomes operational. Even smart dogs don't go straight to college from kindergarten!

Just as there are events geared to certain types of dogs, so there are ones that are more appealing to certain types of people. In some

128

activities, you give the commands and your dog does the work (upland game hunting is one example), while in others, such as agility, you'll both get a workout. You may want to aim for prestigious titles to add to your dog's name, or you may want nothing more than the sheer enjoyment of being around other people and their dogs. Passive or active, participation has its own rewards.

Consider your dog's physical capabilities when looking into any of the canine activities. It's easy to see that a Basset Hound is not built for the racetrack, nor would a Chihuahua be the breed of choice for pulling a sled. A loyal dog will attempt almost anything you ask him to do, so it is up to you to know your dog's limitations. A dog must be physically sound in order to compete at any level in athletic activities, and being mentally sound is a definite plus. Advanced age, however, may not be a deterrent. Many dogs still hunt and herd at ten or twelve years of age. It's entirely possible for dogs to be "fit at 50." Take your dog for a checkup, explain to your vet the type of activity you have in mind and be guided by his or her findings.

All dogs seem to love playing flyball.

You needn't be restricted to breed-specific sports if it's only fun you're after. Certain AKC activities are limited to designated breeds; however, as each new trial, test or sport has grown in popularity, so has the variety of breeds encouraged to participate at a fun level.

But don't shortchange your fun, or that of your dog, by thinking only of the basic function of her breed. Once a dog has learned how to learn, she can be taught to do just about anything as long as the size of the dog is right for the job and you both think it is fun and rewarding. In other words, you are a team.

To get involved in any of the activities detailed in this chapter, look for the names and addresses of the organizations that sponsor them in Chapter 13. You can also ask your breeder or a local dog trainer for contacts.

You can compete in obedience trials with a well trained dog.

Official American Kennel Club Activities

The following tests and trials are some of the events sanctioned by the AKC and sponsored by various dog clubs. Your dog's expertise will be rewarded with impressive titles. You can participate just for fun, or be competitive and go for those awards.

OBEDIENCE

Training classes begin with pups as young as three months of age in kindergarten puppy training, then advance to pre-novice (all exercises on lead) and go on to novice, which is where you'll start off-lead work. In obedience classes dogs learn to sit, stay, heel and come through a variety of exercises. Once you've got the basics down, you can enter obedience trials and work toward earning your dog's first degree, a C.D. (Companion Dog).

The next level is called "Open," in which jumps and retrieves perk up the dog's interest. Passing grades in competition at this level earn a C.D.X. (Companion Dog Excellent). Beyond that lies the goal of the most ambitious—Utility (U.D. and even U.D.X. or OTCh, an Obedience Champion).

AGILITY

All dogs can participate in the latest canine sport to have gained worldwide popularity for its fun and excitement, agility. It began in England as a canine version of horse show-jumping, but because dogs are more agile and able to perform on verbal commands, extra feats were added such as climbing, balancing and racing through tunnels or in and out of weave poles. Many of the obstacles (regulation or homemade) can be set up in your own backyard. If the agility bug bites, you could end up in international competition!

For starters, your dog should be obedience trained, even though, in the beginning, the lessons may all be taught on lead. Once the dog understands the commands (and you do, too), it's as easy as guiding the dog over a prescribed course, one obstacle at a time. In competition, the race is against the clock, so wear your running shoes! The dog starts with 200 points and the judge deducts for infractions and misadventures along the way.

All dogs seem to love agility and respond to it as if they were being turned loose in a playground paradise. Your dog's enthusiasm will be contagious; agility turns into great fun for dog and owner.

FIELD TRIALS AND HUNTING TESTS

There are field trials and hunting tests for the sporting breeds—retrievers, spaniels and pointing breeds, and for some hounds—Bassets, Beagles and Dachshunds. Field trials are competitive events that test a dog's ability to perform the functions for which she was bred. Hunting tests, which are open to retrievers,

---

TITLES AWARDED BY THE AKC

Conformation: Ch. (Champion)

Obedience: CD (Companion Dog); CDX (Companion Dog Excellent); UD (Utility Dog); UDX (Utility Dog Excellent); OTCh. (Obedience Trial Champion)

Field: JH (Junior Hunter); SH (Senior Hunter); MH (Master Hunter); AFCh. (Amateur Field Champion); FCh (Field Champion)

Lure Coursing: JC (Junior Courser); SC (Senior Courser)

Herding: HT (Herding Tested); PT (Pre-Trial Tested); HS (Herding Started); HI (Herding Intermediate); HX (Herding Excellent); HCh. (Herding Champion)

Tracking: TD (Tracking Dog); TDX (Tracking Dog Excellent)

Agility: NAD (Novice Agility); OAD (Open Agility); ADX (Agility Excellent); MAX (Master Agility)

Earthdog Tests: JE (Junior Earthdog); SE (Senior Earthdog); ME (Master Earthdog)

Canine Good Citizen: CGC

Combination: DC (Dual Champion—Ch. and Fch.); TC (Triple Champion—Ch., Fch., and OTCh.)

---

spaniels and pointing breeds only, are noncompetitive and are a means of judging the dog's ability as well as that of the handler.

Hunting is a very large and complex part of canine sports, and if you own one of the breeds that hunts, the events are a great treat for your dog and you. He gets to do what he was bred for, and you get to work with him and watch him do it. You'll be proud of and amazed at what your dog can do.

Fortunately, the AKC publishes a series of booklets on these events, which outline the rules and regulations and include a glossary of the sometimes complicated terms. The AKC also publishes newsletters for field trialers and hunting test enthusiasts. The United Kennel Club (UKC) also has informative materials for the hunter and his dog.

Retrievers and other sporting breeds get to do what they're bred to in hunting tests.

HERDING TESTS AND TRIALS

Herding, like hunting, dates back to the first known uses man made of dogs. The interest in herding today is widespread, and if you own a herding breed, you can join in the activity. Herding dogs are tested for their natural skills to keep a flock of ducks, sheep or cattle together. If your dog shows potential, you can start at the testing level, where your dog can earn a title for showing an inherent herding ability. With training you can advance to the trial level, where your dog should be capable of controlling even difficult livestock in diverse situations.

LURE COURSING

The AKC Tests and Trials for Lure Coursing are open to traditional sighthounds—Greyhounds, Whippets,

Borzoi, Salukis, Afghan Hounds, Ibizan Hounds and Scottish Deerhounds—as well as to Basenjis and Rhodesian Ridgebacks. Hounds are judged on overall ability, follow, speed, agility and endurance. This is possibly the most exciting of the trials for spectators, because the speed and agility of the dogs is awesome to watch as they chase the lure (or "course") in heats of two or three dogs at a time.

TRACKING

Tracking is another activity in which almost any dog can compete because every dog that sniffs the ground when taken outdoors is, in fact, tracking. The hard part comes when the rules as to what, when and where the dog tracks are determined by a person, not the dog! Tracking tests cover a large area of fields, woods and roads. The tracks are

laid hours before the dogs go to work on them, and include "tricks" like cross-tracks and sharp turns. If you're interested in search-and-rescue work, this is the place to start.

This tracking dog is hot on the trail.

EARTHDOG TESTS FOR SMALL TERRIERS AND DACHSHUNDS

These tests are open to Australian, Bedlington, Border, Cairn, Dandie Dinmont, Smooth and Wire Fox, Lakeland, Norfolk, Norwich, Scottish, Sealyham, Skye, Welsh and West Highland White Terriers as well as Dachshunds. The dogs need no prior training for this terrier sport. There is a qualifying test on the day of the event, so dog and handler learn the rules on the spot. These tests, or "digs," sometimes end with informal races in the late afternoon.

Here are some of the extracurricular obedience and racing activities that are not regulated by the AKC or UKC, but are generally run by clubs or a group of dog fanciers and are often open to all.

Canine Freestyle This activity is something new on the scene and is variously likened to dancing, dressage or ice skating. It is meant to show the athleticism of the dog, but also requires showmanship on the part of the dog's handler. If you and your dog like to ham it up for friends, you might want to look into freestyle.

Lure coursing lets sighthounds do what they do best—run!

Scent Hurdle Racing Scent hurdle racing is purely a fun activity sponsored by obedience clubs with members forming competing teams. The height of the hurdles is based on the size of the shortest dog on the team. On a signal, one team dog is released on each of two side-by-side courses and must clear every hurdle before picking up its own dumbbell from a platform and returning over the jumps to the handler. As each dog returns, the next on that team is sent. Of course, that is what the dogs are supposed to do. When the dogs improvise (going under or around the hurdles, stealing another dog's dumbbell, and so forth), it no doubt frustrates the handlers, but just adds to the fun for everyone else.

Flyball This type of racing is similar, but after negotiating the four hurdles, the dog comes to a flyball box, steps on a lever that releases a tennis ball into the air, catches the ball and returns over the hurdles to the starting point. This game also becomes extremely fun for spectators because the dogs sometimes cheat by catching a ball released by the dog in the next lane. Three titles can be earned—Flyball Dog (F.D.), Flyball Dog Excellent (F.D.X.) and Flyball Dog Champion (Fb.D.Ch.)—all awarded by the North American Flyball Association, Inc.

Dogsledding The name conjures up the Rocky Mountains or the frigid North, but you can find dogsled clubs in such unlikely spots as Maryland, North Carolina and Virginia! Dogsledding is primarily for the Nordic breeds such as the Alaskan Malamutes, Siberian Huskies and Samoyeds, but other breeds can try. There are some practical backyard applications to this sport, too. With parental supervision, almost any strong dog could pull a child's sled.

Coming over the A-frame on an agility course.

These are just some of the many recreational ways you can get to know and understand your multifaceted dog better and have fun doing it.

chapter 10

Your Dog
and your
Family

by Bardi McLennan

Adding a dog automatically increases your family by one, no matter whether you live alone in an apartment or are part of a mother, father and six kids household. The single-person family is fair game for numerous and varied canine misconceptions as to who is dog and who pays the bills, whereas a dog in a houseful of children will consider himself to be just one of the gang, littermates all. One dog and one child may give a dog reason to believe they are both kids or both dogs.

Either interpretation requires parental supervision and sometimes speedy intervention.

As soon as one paw goes through the door into your home, Rufus (or Rufina) has to make many adjustments to become a part of your family. Your job is to make him fit in as painlessly as possible. An older dog may have some frame of reference from past experience, but to a 10-week-old puppy, everything is brand new: people, furniture, stairs, when and where people eat, sleep or watch TV, his own place and everyone else's space, smells, sounds, outdoors—everything!

Puppies, and newly acquired dogs of any age, do not need what we think of as "freedom." If you leave a new dog or puppy loose in the house, you will almost certainly return to chaotic destruction and the dog will forever after equate your homecoming with a time of punishment to be dreaded. It is unfair to give your dog what amounts to "freedom to get into trouble." Instead, confine him to a crate for brief periods of your absence (up to three or four hours) and, for the long haul, a workday for example, confine him to one untrashable area with his own toys, a bowl of water and a radio left on (low) in another room.

Lots of pets get along with each other just fine.

For the first few days, when not confined, put Rufus on a long leash tied to your wrist or waist. This umbilical cord method enables the dog to learn all about you from your body language and voice, and to learn by his own actions which things in the house are NO! and which ones are rewarded by "Good dog." House-training will be easier with the pup always by your side. Speaking of which, accidents do happen. That goal of "completely housetrained" takes up to a year, or the length of time it takes the pup to mature.

The All-Adult Family

Most dogs in an adults-only household today are likely to be latchkey pets, with no one home all day but the dog. When you return after a tough day on the job, the dog can and should be your relaxation therapy. But going home can instead be a daily frustration.

Separation anxiety is a very common problem for the dog in a working household. It may begin with whines and barks of loneliness, but it will soon escalate into a frenzied destruction derby. That is why it is so important to set aside the time to teach a dog to relax when left alone in his confined area and to understand that he can trust you to return.

Let the dog get used to your work schedule in easy stages. Confine him to one room and go in and out of that room over and over again. Be casual about it. No physical, voice or eye contact. When the pup no longer even notices your comings and goings, leave the house for varying lengths of time, returning to stay home for a few minutes and gradually increasing the time away. This training can take days, but the dog is learning that you haven't left him forever and that he can trust you.

Any time you leave the dog, but especially during this training period, be casual about your departure. No anxiety-building fond farewells. Just "Bye" and go! Remember the "Good dog" when you return to find everything more or less as you left it.

If things are a mess (or even a disaster) when you return, greet the dog, take him outside to eliminate, and then put him in his crate while you clean up. Rant and rave in the shower! *Do not* punish the dog. You were not there when it happened, and the rule is: Only punish as you catch the dog in the act of wrongdoing. Obviously, it makes sense to get your latchkey puppy when you'll have a week or two to spend on these training essentials.

Family weekend activities should include Rufus whenever possible. Depending on the pup's age, now is the time for a long walk in the park, playtime in the backyard, a hike in the woods. Socializing is as important as health care, good food and physical exercise, so visiting Aunt Emma or Uncle Harry and the next-door neighbor's dog or cat is essential to developing an out-going, friendly temperament in your pet.

If you are a single adult, socializing Rufus at home and away will prevent him from becoming overly protective of you (or just overly attached) and will also prevent such behavioral problems as dominance or fear of strangers.

Babies

Whether already here or on the way, babies figure larger than life in the eyes of a dog. If the dog is there first, let him in on all your baby preparations in the house. When baby arrives, let Rufus sniff any item of clothing that has been on the baby before Junior comes home. Then let Mom greet the dog first before introducing the new family member. Hold the baby down for the dog to see and sniff, but make sure some-one's holding the dog on lead in case of any sudden moves. Don't play keep-away or tease the dog with the baby, which only invites undesirable jump-ing up.

The dog and the baby are "family," and for starters can be treated almost as equals. Things rapidly change, however, espe-cially when baby takes to creeping around on all fours on the dog's turf or, better yet, has yummy pudding all over her face and hands! That's when a lot of things in the dog's and baby's lives become more separate than equal.

Dogs are perfect confidants.

Toddlers make terrible dog owners, but if you can't avoid the combination, use patient discipline (that is, positive teaching rather than punishment), and use time-outs before you run out of patience.

A dog and a baby (or toddler, or an assertive young child) should never be left alone together. Take the dog with you or confine him. With a baby or youngsters in the house, you'll have plenty of use for that wonderful canine safety device called a crate!

Young Children

Any dog in a house with kids will behave pretty much as the kids do, good or bad. But even good dogs and good children can get into trouble when play becomes rowdy and active.

Teach children how to play nicely with a puppy.

Legs bobbing up and down, shrill voices screeching, a ball hurtling overhead, all add up to exuberant frustration for a dog who's just trying to be part of the gang. In a pack of puppies, any legs or toys being chased would be caught by a set of teeth, and all the pups involved would understand that is how the game is played. Kids do not understand this, nor do parents tolerate it. Bring Rufus indoors before you have reason to regret it. This is time-out, not a punishment.

You can explain the situation to the children and tell them they must play quieter games until the puppy learns not to grab them with his mouth. Unfortunately, you can't explain it that easily to the dog. With adult supervision, they will learn how to play together.

Young children love to tease. Sticking their faces or wiggling their hands or fingers in the dog's face is teasing. To another person it might be just annoying, but it is threatening to a dog. There's another difference: We can make the child stop by an explanation, but the only way a dog can stop it is with a warning growl and then with teeth. Teasing is the major cause of children being bitten by their pets. Treat it seriously.

Older Children

The best age for a child to get a first dog is between the ages of 8 and 12. That's when kids are able to accept some real responsibility for their pet. Even so, take the child's vow of "I will never *ever* forget to feed (brush, walk, etc.) the dog" for what it's worth: a child's good intention at that moment. Most kids today have extra lessons, soccer practice, Little League, ballet, and so forth piled on top of school schedules. There will be many times when Mom will have to come to the dog's rescue. "I walked the dog for you so you can set the table for me" is one way to get around a missed appointment without laying on blame or guilt.

Kids in this age group make excellent obedience trainers because they are into the teaching/learning process themselves and they lack the self-consciousness of adults. Attending a dog show is something the whole family can enjoy, and watching Junior Showmanship may catch the eye of the kids. Older children can begin to get involved in many of the recreational activities that were reviewed in the previous chapter. Some of the agility obstacles, for example, can be set up in the backyard as a family project (with an adult making sure all the equipment is safe and secure for the dog).

Older kids are also beginning to look to the future, and may envision themselves as veterinarians or trainers or show dog handlers or writers of the next Lassie best-seller. Dogs are perfect confidants for these dreams. They won't tell a soul.

Other Pets

Introduce all pets tactfully. In a dog/cat situation, hold the dog, not the cat. Let two dogs meet on neutral turf—a stroll in the park or a walk down the street—with both on loose leads to permit all the normal canine ways of saying hello, including routine sniffing, circling, more sniffing, and so on. Small creatures such as hamsters, chinchillas or mice must be kept safe from their natural predators (dogs and cats).

Festive Family Occasions

Parties are great for people, but not necessarily for puppies. Until all the guests have arrived, put the dog in his crate or in a room where he won't be disturbed. A socialized dog can join the fun later as long as he's not underfoot, annoying guests or into the hors d'oeuvres.

There are a few dangers to consider, too. Doors opening and closing can allow a puppy to slip out unnoticed in the confusion, and you'll be organizing a search party instead of playing host or hostess. Party food and buffet service are not for dogs. Let Rufus party in his crate with a nice big dog biscuit.

At Christmas time, not only are tree decorations dangerous and breakable (and perhaps family heirlooms), but extreme caution should be taken with the lights, cords and outlets for the tree lights and any other festive lighting. Occasionally a dog lifts a leg, ignoring the fact that the tree is indoors. To avoid this, use a canine repellent, made for gardens, on the tree. Or keep him out of the tree room unless supervised. And whatever you do, *don't* invite trouble by hanging his toys on the tree!

Car Travel

Before you plan a vacation by car or RV with Rufus, be sure he enjoys car travel. Nothing spoils a holiday quicker than a carsick dog! Work within the dog's comfort level. Get in the car with the dog in his crate or attached to a canine car safety belt and just sit there until he relaxes. That's all. Next time, get in the car, turn on the engine and go nowhere. Just sit. When that is okay, turn on the engine and go around the block. Now you can go for a ride and include a stop where you get out, leaving the dog for a minute or two.

On a warm day, always park in the shade and leave windows open several inches. And return quickly. It only takes 10 minutes for a car to become an overheated steel death trap.

Motel or Pet Motel?

Not all motels or hotels accept pets, but you have a much better choice today than even a few years ago. To find a dog-friendly lodging, look at *On the Road Again With Man's Best Friend*, a series of directories that detail bed and breakfasts, inns, family resorts and other hotels/motels. Some places require a refundable deposit to cover any damage incurred by the dog. More B&Bs accept pets now, but some restrict the size.

If taking Rufus with you is not feasible, check out boarding kennels in your area. Your veterinarian may offer this service, or recommend a kennel or two he or she is familiar with. Go see the facilities for yourself, ask about exercise, diet, housing, and so on. Or, if you'd rather have Rufus stay home, look into bonded petsitters, many of whom will also bring in the mail and water your plants.

chapter 11

Your Dog
and your
Community

by Bardi McLennan

Step outside your home with your dog and you are no longer just family, you are both part of your community. This is when the phrase "responsible pet ownership" takes on serious implications. For starters, it means you pick up after your dog—not just occasionally, but every time your dog eliminates away from home. That means you have joined the Plastic Baggy Brigade! You always have plastic sandwich bags in your pocket and several in the car. It means you teach your kids how to use them, too. If you think this is "yucky," just imagine what the person (a non-doggy person) who inadvertently steps in the mess thinks!

Your responsibility extends to your neighbors: To their ears (no annoying barking); to their property (their garbage, their lawn, their flower beds, their cat— especially their cat); to their kids (on bikes, at play); to their kids' toys and sports equipment.

There are numerous dog-related laws, ranging from simple dog licensing and leash laws to those holding you liable for any physical injury or property damage done by your dog. These laws are in place to protect everyone in the community, including you and your dog. There are town ordinances and state laws which are by no means the same in all towns or all states. Ignorance of the law won't get you off the hook. The time to find out what the laws are where you live is now.

Be sure your dog's license is current. This is not just a good local ordinance, it can make the difference between finding your lost dog or not. Many states now require proof of rabies vaccination and that the dog has been spayed or neutered before issuing a license. At the same time, keep up the dog's annual immunizations.

Dressing your dog up makes him appealing to strangers.

Never let your dog run loose in the neighborhood. This will not only keep you on the right side of the leash law, it's the outdoor version of the rule about not giving your dog "freedom to get into trouble."

Good Canine Citizen

Sometimes it's hard for a dog's owner to assess whether or not the dog is sufficiently socialized to be accepted by the community at large. Does Rufus or Rufina display good, controlled behavior in public? The AKC's Canine Good Citizen program is available through many dog organizations. If your dog passes the test, the title "CGC" is earned.

The overall purpose is to turn your dog into a good neighbor and to teach you about your responsibility to your community as a dog owner. Here are the ten things your dog must do willingly:

1. Accept a stranger stopping to chat with you.
2. Sit and be petted by a stranger.
3. Allow a stranger to handle him or her as a groomer or veterinarian would.
4. Walk nicely on a loose lead.
5. Walk calmly through a crowd.
6. Sit and down on command, then stay in a sit or down position while you walk away.
7. Come when called.
8. Casually greet another dog.
9. React confidently to distractions.
10. Accept being left alone with someone other than you and not become overly agitated or nervous.

Schools and Dogs

Schools are getting involved with pet ownership on an educational level. It has been proven that children who are kind to animals are humane in their attitude toward other people as adults.

A dog is a child's best friend, and so children are often primary pet owners, if not the primary caregivers. Unfortunately, they are also the ones most often bitten by dogs. This occurs due to a lack of understanding that pets, no matter how sweet, cuddly and loving, are still animals. Schools, along with parents, dog clubs, dog fanciers and the AKC, are working to change all that with video programs for children not only in grade school, but in the nursery school and pre-kindergarten age group. Teaching youngsters how to be responsible dog owners is important community work. When your dog has a CGC, volunteer to take part in an educational classroom event put on by your dog club.

Boy Scout Merit Badge

A Merit Badge for Dog Care can be earned by any Boy Scout ages 11 to 18. The requirements are not easy, but amount to a complete course in responsible dog care and general ownership. Here are just a few of the things a Scout must do to earn that badge:

> Point out ten parts of the dog using the correct names.
>
> Give a report (signed by parent or guardian) on your care of the dog (feeding, food used, housing, exercising, grooming and bathing), plus what has been done to keep the dog healthy.
>
> Explain the right way to obedience train a dog, and demonstrate three comments.
>
> Several of the requirements have to do with health care, including first aid, handling a hurt dog, and the dangers of home treatment for a serious ailment.
>
> The final requirement is to know the local laws and ordinances involving dogs.

There are similar programs for Girl Scouts and 4-H members.

Local Clubs

Local dog clubs are no longer in existence just to put on a yearly dog show. Today, they are apt to be the hub of the community's involvement with pets. Dog clubs conduct educational forums with big-name speakers, stage demonstrations of canine talent in a busy mall and take dogs of various breeds to schools for classroom discussion.

The quickest way to feel accepted as a member in a club is to volunteer your services! Offer to help with something—anything—and watch your popularity (and your interest) grow.

Therapy Dogs

Once your dog has earned that essential CGC and reliably demonstrates a steady, calm temperament, you could look into what therapy dogs are doing in your area.

Therapy dogs go with their owners to visit patients at hospitals or nursing homes, generally remaining on leash but able to coax a pat from a stiffened hand, a smile from a blank face, a few words from sealed lips or a hug from someone in need of love.

Your dog can make a differ-ence in lots of lives.

Nursing homes cover a wide range of patient care. Some specialize in care of the elderly, some in the treatment of specific illnesses, some in physical therapy. Children's facilities also welcome visits from trained therapy dogs for boosting morale in their pediatric patients. Hospice care for the terminally ill and the at-home care of AIDS patients are other areas where this canine visiting is desperately needed. Therapy dog training comes first.

There is a lot more involved than just taking your nice friendly pooch to someone's bedside. Doing therapy dog work involves your own emotional stability as well as that of your dog. But once you have met all the requirements for this work, making the rounds once a week or once a month with your therapy dog is possibly the most rewarding of all community activities.

Disaster Aid

This community service is definitely not for everyone, partly because it is time-consuming. The initial training is rigorous, and there can be no let-up in the continuing workouts, because members are on call 24 hours a day to go wherever they are needed at a moment's notice. But if you think you would like to be able to assist in a disaster, look into search-and-rescue work. The network of search-and-rescue volunteers is worldwide, and all members of the American Rescue Dog Association (ARDA) who are qualified to do this work are volunteers who train and maintain their own dogs.

Physical Aid

Most people are familiar with Seeing Eye dogs, which serve as blind people's eyes, but not with all the other work that dogs are trained to do to assist the disabled. Dogs are also specially trained to pull wheelchairs, carry school books, pick up dropped objects, open and close doors. Some also are cars for the deaf. All these assistance-trained dogs, by the way, are allowed anywhere "No Pet" signs exist (as are therapy dogs when

properly identified). Getting started in any of this fascinating work requires a background in dog training and canine behavior, but there are also volunteer jobs ranging from answering the phone to cleaning out kennels to providing a foster home for a puppy. You have only to ask.

Making the rounds with your therapy dog can be very rewarding.

part four

Beyond
the
Basics

chapter 12

Recommended Reading

Books

About Health Care

Ackerman, Lowell. *Guide to Skin and Haircoat Problems in Dogs.* Loveland, Colo.: Alpine Publications, 1994.

Alderton, David. *The Dog Care Manual.* Hauppauge, N.Y.: Barron's Educational Series, Inc., 1986.

American Kennel Club. *American Kennel Club Dog Care and Training.* New York: Howell Book House, 1991.

Bamberger, Michelle, DVM. *Help! The Quick Guide to First Aid for Your Dog.* New York: Howell Book House, 1995.

Carlson, Delbert, DVM, and James Giffin, MD. *Dog Owner's Home Veterinary Handbook.* New York: Howell Book House, 1992.

DeBitetto, James, DVM, and Sarah Hodgson. *You & Your Puppy.* New York: Howell Book House, 1995.

Humphries, Jim, DVM. *Dr. Jim's Animal Clinic for Dogs.* New York: Howell Book House, 1994.

McGinnis, Terri. *The Well Dog Book.* New York: Random House, 1991.

Pitcairn, Richard and Susan. *Natural Health for Dogs.* Emmaus, Pa.: Rodale Press, 1982.

About Dog Shows

Hall, Lynn. *Dog Showing for Beginners.* New York: Howell Book House, 1994.

Nichols, Virginia Tuck. *How to Show Your Own Dog.* Neptune, N. J.: TFH, 1970.

Vanacore, Connie. *Dog Showing, An Owner's Guide.* New York: Howell Book House, 1990.

ABOUT TRAINING

Ammen, Amy. *Training in No Time.* New York: Howell Book House, 1995.

Baer, Ted. *Communicating With Your Dog.* Hauppauge, N.Y.: Barron's Educational Series, Inc., 1989.

Benjamin, Carol Lea. *Dog Problems.* New York: Howell Book House, 1989.

Benjamin, Carol Lea. *Dog Training for Kids.* New York: Howell Book House, 1988.

Benjamin, Carol Lea. *Mother Knows Best.* New York: Howell Book House, 1985.

Benjamin, Carol Lea. *Surviving Your Dog's Adolescence.* New York: Howell Book House, 1993.

Bohnenkamp, Gwen. *Manners for the Modern Dog.* San Francisco: Perfect Paws, 1990.

Dibra, Bashkim. *Dog Training by Bash.* New York: Dell, 1992.

Dunbar, Ian, PhD, MRCVS. *Dr. Dunbar's Good Little Dog Book,* James & Kenneth Publishers, 2140 Shattuck Ave. #2406, Berkeley, Calif. 94704. (510) 658–8588. Order from the publisher.

Dunbar, Ian, PhD, MRCVS. *How to Teach a New Dog Old Tricks,* James & Kenneth Publishers. Order from the publisher; address above.

Dunbar, Ian, PhD, MRCVS, and Gwen Bohnenkamp. Booklets on *Preventing Aggression; Housetraining; Chewing; Digging; Barking; Socialization; Fearfulness; and Fighting,* James & Kenneth Publishers. Order from the publisher; address above.

Evans, Job Michael. *People, Pooches and Problems.* New York: Howell Book House, 1991.

Kilcommons, Brian and Sarah Wilson. *Good Owners, Great Dogs.* New York: Warner Books, 1992.

McMains, Joel M. *Dog Logic—Companion Obedience.* New York: Howell Book House, 1992.

Rutherford, Clarice and David H. Neil, MRCVS. *How to Raise a Puppy You Can Live With.* Loveland, Colo.: Alpine Publications, 1982.

Volhard, Jack and Melissa Bartlett. *What All Good Dogs Should Know: The Sensible Way to Train.* New York: Howell Book House, 1991.

ABOUT BREEDING

Harris, Beth J. Finder. *Breeding a Litter, The Complete Book of Prenatal and Postnatal Care.* New York: Howell Book House, 1983.

Holst, Phyllis, DVM. *Canine Reproduction.* Loveland, Colo.: Alpine Publications, 1985.

Walkowicz, Chris and Bonnie Wilcox, DVM. *Successful Dog Breeding, The Complete Handbook of Canine Midwifery.* New York: Howell Book House, 1994.

ABOUT ACTIVITIES

American Rescue Dog Association. *Search and Rescue Dogs.* New York: Howell Book House, 1991.

Barwig, Susan and Stewart Hilliard. *Schutzhund.* New York: Howell Book House, 1991.

Beaman, Arthur S. *Lure Coursing.* New York: Howell Book House, 1994.

Daniels, Julie. *Enjoying Dog Agility—From Backyard to Competition.* New York: Doral Publishing, 1990.

Davis, Kathy Diamond. *Therapy Dogs.* New York: Howell Book House, 1992.

Gallup, Davis Anne. *Running With Man's Best Friend.* Loveland, Colo.: Alpine Publications, 1986.

Habgood, Dawn and Robert. *On the Road Again With Man's Best Friend.* New England, Mid-Atlantic, West Coast and Southeast editions. Selective guides to area bed and breakfasts, inns, hotels and resorts that welcome guests and their dogs. New York. Howell Book House, 1995.

Holland, Vergil S. *Herding Dogs.* New York: Howell Book House, 1994.

LaBelle, Charlene G. *Backpacking With Your Dog.* Loveland, Colo.: Alpine Publications, 1993.

Simmons-Moake, Jane. *Agility Training, The Fun Sport for All Dogs.* New York: Howell Book House, 1991.

Spencer, James B. *Hup! Training Flushing Spaniels the American Way.* New York: Howell Book House, 1992.

Spencer, James B. *Point! Training the All-Seasons Birddog.* New York: Howell Book House, 1995.

Tarrant, Bill. *Training the Hunting Retriever.* New York: Howell Book House, 1991.

Volhard, Jack and Wendy. *The Canine Good Citizen.* New York: Howell Book House, 1994.

General Titles

Haggerty, Captain Arthur J. *How to Get Your Pet Into Show Business.* New York: Howell Book House, 1994.

McLennan, Bardi. *Dogs and Kids, Parenting Tips.* New York: Howell Book House, 1993.

Moran, Patti J. *Pet Sitting for Profit, A Complete Manual for Professional Success.* New York: Howell Book House, 1992.

Scalisi, Danny and Libby Moses. *When Rover Just Won't Do, Over 2,000 Suggestions for Naming Your Dog.* New York: Howell Book House, 1993.

Sife, Wallace, PhD. *The Loss of a Pet.* New York: Howell Book House, 1993.

Wrede, Barbara J. *Civilizing Your Puppy.* Hauppauge, N.Y.: Barron's Educational Series, 1992.

Magazines

The AKC GAZETTE, The Official Journal for the Sport of Purebred Dogs. American Kennel Club, 51 Madison Ave., New York, NY.

Bloodlines Journal. United Kennel Club, 100 E. Kilgore Rd., Kalamazoo, MI.

Dog Fancy. Fancy Publications, 3 Burroughs, Irvine, CA 92718

Dog World. Maclean Hunter Publishing Corp., 29 N. Wacker Dr., Chicago, IL 60606.

Videos

"SIRIUS Puppy Training," by Ian Dunbar, PhD, MRCVS. James & Kenneth Publishers, 2140 Shattuck Ave. #2406, Berkeley, CA 94704. Order from the publisher.

"Training the Companion Dog," from Dr. Dunbar's British TV Series, James & Kenneth Publishers. (See address above).

The American Kennel Club produces videos on every breed of dog, as well as on hunting tests, field trials and other areas of interest to purebred dog owners. For more information, write to AKC/Video Fulfillment, 5580 Centerview Dr., Suite 200, Raleigh, NC 27606.

chapter 13

Resources

Breed Clubs

Every breed recognized by the American Kennel Club has a national (parent) club. National clubs are a great source of information on your breed. You can get the name of the secretary of the club by contacting:

The American Kennel Club
51 Madison Avenue
New York, NY 10010
(212) 696-8200

There are also numerous all-breed, individual breed, obedience, hunting and other special-interest dog clubs across the country. The American Kennel Club can provide you with a geographical list of clubs to find ones in your area. Contact them at the above address.

Registry Organizations

Registry organizations register purebred dogs. The American Kennel Club is the oldest and largest in this country, and currently recognizes over 130 breeds. The United Kennel Club registers some breeds the AKC doesn't (including the American Pit Bull Terrier and the Miniature Fox Terrier) as well as many of the same breeds. The others included here are for your reference; the AKC can provide you with a list of foreign registries.

American Kennel Club
51 Madison Avenue
New York, NY 10010

United Kennel Club (UKC)
100 E. Kilgore Road
Kalamazoo, MI 49001-5598

American Dog Breeders Assn.
P.O. Box 1771
Salt Lake City, UT 84110
(Registers American Pit Bull Terriers)

Canadian Kennel Club
89 Skyway Avenue
Etobicoke, Ontario
Canada M9W 6R4

National Stock Dog Registry
P.O. Box 402
Butler, IN 46721
(Registers working stock dogs)

Orthopedic Foundation for Animals (OFA)
2300 E. Nifong Blvd.
Columbia, MO 65201-3856
(Hip registry)

Activity Clubs

Write to these organizations for information on the activities they sponsor.

American Kennel Club
51 Madison Avenue
New York, NY 10010
(Conformation Shows, Obedience Trials, Field Trials and Hunting Tests, Agility, Canine Good

Citizen, Lure Coursing, Herding, Tracking,
Earthdog Tests, Coonhunting.)

United Kennel Club
100 E. Kilgore Road
Kalamazoo, MI 49001-5598
(Conformation Shows, Obedience Trials, Agility,
Hunting for Various Breeds, Terrier Trials and
more.)

North American Flyball Assn.
1342 Jeff St.
Ypsilanti, MI 48198

International Sled Dog Racing Assn.
P.O. Box 446
Norman, ID 83848-0446

North American Working Dog Assn., Inc.
Southeast Kreisgruppe
P.O. Box 833
Brunswick, GA 31521

Trainers

Association of Pet Dog Trainers
P.O. Box 385
Davis, CA 95617
(800) PET–DOGS

American Dog Trainers' Network
161 West 4th St.
New York, NY 10014
(212) 727–7257

**National Association of Dog Obedience
Instructors**
2286 East Steel Rd.
St. Johns, MI 48879

Associations

American Dog Owners Assn.
1654 Columbia Tpk.
Castleton, NY 12033
(Combats anti-dog legislation)

Delta Society
P.O. Box 1080
Renton, WA 98057-1080
(Promotes the human/animal bond through
pet-assisted therapy and other programs)

Dog Writers Assn. of America (DWAA)
Sally Cooper, Secy.
222 Woodchuck Ln.
Harwinton, CT 06791

National Assn. for Search and Rescue (NASAR)
P.O. Box 3709
Fairfax, VA 22038

Therapy Dogs International
6 Hilltop Road
Mendham, NJ 07945